Show Up More Financially

A Simple Guide to Ending Money Stress and Building Lasting Peace

Jim Sabellico

ONE

Introduction

If you've ever looked at your life and thought, *I work too hard to still feel this way about money,* you're not alone.

Maybe you make good money but can't shake the pressure that comes with it. Maybe you're always chasing more but never feel secure. Maybe you find yourself checking your accounts a dozen times a week, or avoiding them altogether because you're tired of what they reveal. Or maybe, deep down, you know that money has started to control you more than you'd like to admit.

Most people aren't bad with money. They're just trapped in unhealthy relationships with it. They treat money like a problem to fix, a god to serve, or a goal to conquer. Some feel ruled by scarcity, always worried there won't be enough. Others are ruled by success, always chasing the next milestone. But either way, the outcome is the same. You end up living *for* money instead of letting money work *for* you.

I know that feeling. I've lived in both extremes. There were seasons where I was scraping by and others where the numbers looked great on paper but my peace was gone. The common thread wasn't the amount in my account. It was how I thought about it, how I used it, and how much power I gave it.

This book isn't about becoming rich. It's about becoming free. Free from the anxiety of not knowing where your money goes. Free from the guilt of spending or the shame of saving too late. Free from the idea that your value is tied to your balance sheet.

Showing up financially means learning to lead your money with purpose instead of reacting to it with fear. It's about gaining clarity, not just in your budget, but in your beliefs. It's about understanding that money is a tool, not a master. And it's about building systems that give you peace instead of pressure.

We'll talk about the practical things: how to pay yourself first, how to budget without hating it, how to build wealth that grows even when you sleep. But we'll also talk about the personal side: the stories you inherited, the habits that keep you stuck, and the mindset that finally sets you free.

You don't need a finance degree or a perfect record. You just need a willingness to be honest about where you are and courage to start changing it. Step by step, you'll learn how to make money serve your life instead of shape it.

Because the truth is, financial health isn't just about numbers. It's about peace. It's about having control without obsession. It's about being able to provide, give, save, and rest.

And that's what we're here to build together.

Let's learn what it really means to show up more financially.

TWO

The Silent Master

Money is one of the most powerful forces in your life, and yet it rarely introduces itself honestly.

It doesn't shout its rules or explain its motives. It just moves quietly in the background, shaping decisions, influencing relationships, and guiding what you believe is possible. It tells you when to wake up, when to rest, and how much of yourself to give to the world. It's the silent master most people serve without realizing it.

We learn early that money matters. We're told to work hard, save what we can, and spend wisely. Those ideas sound simple, but the emotions underneath them are not. Somewhere along the way, money stops being a tool and starts becoming a test. We begin to measure our worth by what we earn, our competence by what we own, and our success by how we compare.

Even people who say they do not care about money are often tangled in it. They care about opportunity, about time, about peace of mind. All of those are shaped by money's reach. You can pretend it doesn't matter, but it still whispers in the back of your mind every time you choose between what you want and what you can afford.

I spent years under that quiet influence. I thought I was chasing freedom, but I was really chasing control. I believed that if I could just make enough, the pressure would finally disappear. It never did. The numbers changed, the anxiety didn't. I was measuring progress by income instead of by peace, and peace was always out of reach.

That is what money does when it goes unchecked. It convinces you that relief is just one raise, one deal, or one good month away. But every time you get there, the finish line moves. You buy the relief for a moment, then lose it to the next goal. You work harder, spend faster, and still feel the same quiet tension in your chest.

Money becomes the background noise of your life. It hums through every decision you make, even when you try to ignore it. You tell yourself that you are being practical, that this is what responsible adults do. You grind through jobs you no longer love because stability feels safer than change. You delay rest because the bills won't stop coming. You check your accounts more often than you pray, think, or breathe. You start to believe that the balance on your screen is the scoreboard of your value.

That belief is the reason so many people who have "made it" still feel miserable. They got what they thought they wanted, but they traded too much to keep it. They lost peace for productivity. They gained wealth but never learned how to stop worrying about losing it. They live in houses that echo with stress. They smile in public and lie awake at night wondering why it still feels like not enough.

Money itself is neutral. It doesn't bless or curse. It reflects. It amplifies who you already are. If you are fearful, it feeds that fear. If you are generous, it multiplies your reach. If you are

insecure, it becomes your mirror and your mask
at the same time.

That is why awareness is everything. You cannot
change your relationship with money until you
admit that you already have one. Whether you
struggle with it, chase it, or avoid it, you are in
a relationship with it right now. And like any
relationship, the quality of that connection
determines how much peace you have.

You may not talk about it out loud, but money is
already part of your conversations. It decides
where you live, what you eat, how you spend
your time, and even who you feel comfortable
around. It shapes your self-image. It influences
what you believe you deserve. It even affects
how you see other people.

That is what makes it dangerous. Money can
build entire identities. You start defining
yourself by titles and totals. You introduce
yourself by what you do instead of who you are.
You measure days by productivity instead of
purpose. And slowly, without noticing, you let
the silent master take over your sense of self.

The good news is that you can take it back.

Showing up financially doesn't mean abandoning ambition or pretending money doesn't matter. It means learning how to lead it instead of being led by it. It means deciding that money will have a place in your life, but not the highest one. It means treating it as a servant, not a savior.

You start by noticing where it already holds power. Think about the moments when money controls your emotions. The argument that starts after a bill comes in. The anxiety that hits when a payment is late. The pressure that makes you say yes when you want to say no. Those moments aren't just about dollars. They are about influence.

When you can see that influence clearly, you can start to break it. You stop reacting and start leading. You stop saying, "I can't afford that," and start asking, "Is that where I want my money to go?" You stop letting the silent master dictate your limits and begin setting your own.

Money was never meant to run your life. It was meant to support it. But it only does that when you are willing to look it in the eye. Most people never do. They fear what it might reveal. But the truth is, money reveals everything eventually. It shows your priorities. It shows your values. It shows what matters most.

That revelation isn't meant to shame you. It's meant to wake you up. Once you see how deeply money influences your choices, you can decide how to rewrite that influence. You can choose clarity instead of confusion, stewardship instead of scarcity, purpose instead of panic.

When you start to see money as something you can direct instead of something that directs you, the silence breaks. The weight begins to lift. You start to understand that peace has never been about the amount you have, but about the authority you hold over it.

That is where financial freedom really begins. Not in the size of your paycheck, but in the strength of your perspective.

You are meant to lead your money, not serve it. And once you do, you'll realize that the silent master was never stronger than your awareness. It only had as much power as you were willing to give it.

This is where the shift starts. Awareness first, control second. Because when you finally see what's been running your life, you can start running it better.

That's how you begin to show up more financially.

THREE

The Story Behind Your Spending

Every financial decision tells a story, even the small ones you barely notice. The coffee on the way to work. The cart that fills faster than you planned. The way you feel when you swipe your card, check your balance, or see the total at the gas pump. Every number you move carries emotion behind it. Most people think they are managing money, but what they are really managing is how they feel about it.

Money has never been purely logical. It looks like math, but it moves like memory. It carries the weight of your past and the tone of your fears. Every habit, every purchase, every hesitation comes from somewhere. The problem is that most people never stop long enough to trace it back.

You might believe that you are bad with money, but that is rarely true. You are not careless. You are just acting out the story you were taught.

Some people spend quickly because they grew up without much and learned to grab what they could before it was gone. They treat money like a chance that might disappear if they wait too long. Some hold on tightly because they were raised in scarcity and learned that safety only comes from saving. They think comfort is dangerous because it could lead to loss. Some overwork because they believe earning is the same as proving. They equate value with productivity. And some give too much, not out of generosity, but guilt. They are trying to buy peace, hoping that giving will silence the part of them that still feels undeserving.

These stories are powerful because they are invisible. They shape your relationship with money long before you realize you have one. You are not consciously choosing them. They are choosing for you.

When I finally started paying attention to my spending, I realized it had nothing to do with discipline. I was repeating a pattern I did not know I had learned. Every financial habit I called normal was actually emotional. The days I avoided looking at my accounts were the days I felt most insecure. The times I spent impulsively were the moments I felt least in control. Money had become my way of regulating emotions I did not know how to name.

That realization was uncomfortable, but it was freeing. It meant that if the problem started in my story, the solution could too.

To change the way you spend, you first have to learn to listen. Your spending habits are trying to tell you something. They reveal where you seek comfort, control, or validation. They show where you are still trying to make up for what you once lacked.

Think about how you feel when you spend money. Do you feel relief or regret? Do you feel guilty when you buy something for yourself, or proud that you resisted? Do you spend to celebrate, to distract, to escape, or to belong? Those small reactions hold clues.

Money always finds its way back to emotion. The act might look physical, but the reason is psychological. You are not buying the thing itself. You are buying the feeling that thing promises to bring.

When you understand that, everything begins to make sense. You start seeing how your habits are less about what you can afford and more about what you believe.

I remember a season where I would spend money on things I did not even want. A meal out. A quick purchase online. It felt harmless, but underneath, I was chasing relief. Each swipe gave me a momentary escape from the pressure of everything else. I called it treating myself. In reality, it was distraction disguised as reward.

Most people have a version of that. Some over-save and call it discipline, but it is really fear of being caught unprepared. Some avoid learning about investing because the idea of making a mistake feels unbearable. Some never spend on themselves because they secretly believe they do not deserve nice things. The actions are different, but the story underneath is the same. It is about safety, identity, and control.

Once you can see that story, you can start rewriting it. Awareness interrupts the pattern. The next time you spend, pause long enough to notice what you are feeling. Are you buying from peace or from pressure? From joy or from stress? From confidence or from fear?

You will not always get it right, but you will start to feel the difference. When spending comes from peace, it feels light. When it comes from fear, it feels heavy.

You will also start to notice how much of your financial life runs on autopilot. The subscriptions you forgot to cancel. The small purchases that blur together. The routines that feel normal but keep you stuck. Seeing them clearly is not about guilt. It is about clarity. You cannot change what you refuse to see.

And when you finally do see it, something begins to shift. You start realizing that managing money is not about restriction. It is about awareness. It is about deciding that your financial story will no longer run in the background without your permission.

That moment of awareness is where personal power returns. You no longer feel like life is happening to you. You begin to feel like you are participating in it. The tension between what you want and what you can afford becomes less emotional and more strategic. You stop chasing the next big fix and start building calm consistency instead.

This is where financial peace begins, not in the numbers but in the narrative. You cannot out-earn a bad story. You have to rewrite it. You have to stop living out the beliefs you inherited and start building the ones that align with the life you want.

When you start paying attention, you learn that money is never random. It is a mirror reflecting your priorities, your fears, and your growth. It tells you what you believe you deserve and what you still think you must prove.

You cannot silence that reflection, but you can change what it shows.

Showing up financially means taking ownership of that story. It means deciding that from this point forward, your spending will serve your peace instead of your past.

Because the truth is, money will always tell a story. The only question is whether it will keep repeating the old one or start telling a new one you actually want to live.

FOUR

Unconscious Debt

There is a kind of debt that doesn't appear on a credit report. It doesn't send statements or charge interest, yet it shapes the way you live. It hides in the background of your choices, showing up in your reactions to money before you even realize it. That is unconscious debt.

It starts forming long before you ever earn a paycheck. You begin collecting it as a child, one experience at a time. You absorb the tone of your parents' voices when bills came due. You notice how they argued about money or never spoke about it at all. You learn what wealth means by how people around you treat it. You

hear the stories whispered through your family
about people who have too much or too little,
and you carry those judgments into adulthood
like quiet instructions.

No one teaches you these things directly. They
seep in through repetition. You learn that some
topics are safe and some are not. You learn that
asking questions makes adults tense. You learn
that being good with money means being
cautious, or that success makes you selfish. You
learn to associate money with pride or pain,
abundance or shame. By the time you are grown,
those lessons have already become part of you.

That is what makes this kind of debt so heavy.
You do not know it exists until you feel its
weight. It sits beneath the surface of your
financial life, pulling on every decision you
make. You work harder to avoid guilt. You save
out of fear rather than purpose. You spend to
fill the emptiness that hard work never seems to
fix. You keep repeating habits that don't make
sense on paper because, emotionally, they still
feel familiar.

When I first began paying attention to my own
financial patterns, I realized how deeply my
upbringing shaped them. I could remember
moments that looked insignificant at the time

but left invisible marks. The nights when my parents whispered about bills after they thought I was asleep. The afternoons when money decided whether we could say yes to something simple. Those moments planted a belief that life was always one bad month away from falling apart. Even when things got better, I never stopped waiting for them to get worse.

That belief followed me into adulthood like a shadow. It influenced every choice I made, from the jobs I took to the way I handled success. I told myself I was being responsible, but really, I was still a child trying to make sure there was enough. I thought I had escaped scarcity, but I had only changed its scenery.

Most people carry some version of this. Maybe you grew up in plenty and learned that money equals control, so you hold it tightly. Maybe you grew up in struggle and learned that money equals worth, so you chase it endlessly. Or maybe you learned that talking about money only creates conflict, so you stay silent and hope things will somehow sort themselves out.

These patterns feel personal, but they are inherited. They were passed down like family heirlooms, not because anyone meant harm, but because that was the only way they knew how to survive. Every generation tries to do better, yet without awareness, we simply repeat.

That is what unconscious debt really costs. It keeps you living by rules that no longer apply. You earn, save, and spend inside a framework that was built for someone else's world. And no matter how hard you work, peace never comes, because the problem isn't your balance. It's the beliefs beneath it.

Breaking free begins with honesty. You have to face the emotional balance sheet of your past. Think about the lessons you were taught about money, not just in words but in feelings. Did it mean security or stress? Was it something to be talked about or hidden? Did success feel earned or suspicious? Those impressions still speak in your decisions today.

When you start to see them clearly, you can finally question them. You begin to ask if those old lessons are still true, or if they were simply true for someone else. You stop letting old fears spend your energy for you.

Awareness alone doesn't erase the past, but it loosens its grip. It helps you see that your story with money began before you could choose it, but it does not have to end that way. You can acknowledge where those beliefs came from without blaming anyone for them. Compassion for the past gives you power in the present.

There is a strange comfort in old financial habits. Even the painful ones can feel safe because they are predictable. They remind you of home, of how things always were. But comfort and health are not the same. Growth means learning to live differently, even when it feels uncomfortable at first.

When you start replacing fear with understanding, something begins to change. You make a budget not as punishment, but as clarity. You save not to hide from the future, but to prepare for it. You spend not to numb yourself, but to enjoy life responsibly. Each small act becomes a way of rewriting the story you inherited.

The moment you stop blaming yourself for what you didn't know, you free yourself to learn what you can. You stop feeling shame for repeating patterns and start feeling gratitude for noticing them. Awareness becomes your first payment toward a different kind of wealth.

Financial health isn't just about making money. It's about making peace with where it came from. It's about seeing the invisible lessons that have shaped your choices and deciding which ones are worth keeping. When you recognize the emotional debt you have been carrying, you can finally stop paying interest on it.

Unconscious debt loses its power the moment you bring it into the light. It can no longer direct your choices from the shadows. You begin to see money as it truly is, not as a symbol of fear or control, but as a resource you can learn to manage with intention.

You cannot rewrite your past, but you can choose how it informs your future. Every step toward financial awareness is a step away from the invisible debts of yesterday. Each time you act with clarity instead of conditioning, you are paying down what you once owed to old beliefs.

That is how you begin to build real wealth. Not just in numbers, but in freedom.

Because the truest kind of financial freedom is not being debt-free on paper. It is being free from the fears that used to decide what your life could look like.

And that freedom begins here, when you finally choose to stop carrying what never belonged to you.

FIVE

Scarcity or Stewardship

For most of my life, I thought being careful with money was the same as being wise. I believed that fear and responsibility were two sides of the same coin. If I was anxious about money, that meant I was paying attention. If I was cautious, that meant I was being smart. It took me years to realize that fear and wisdom may look similar, but they grow from entirely different soil.

Fear comes from scarcity. Wisdom comes from stewardship.

Scarcity is a voice that whispers you will never have enough. It tells you that no matter what you earn, security is always just a little further ahead. It convinces you that life is fragile, that opportunities are rare, and that you must hold tightly to everything you have or risk losing it all. Scarcity makes you compete instead of create. It keeps you running, even when you already have what you once prayed for.

Stewardship sounds quieter, but stronger. It reminds you that what you have is already enough to manage with purpose. It invites gratitude instead of panic. It says that money is not a finish line, it is a resource. It belongs to you for a time, and what you do with it determines how much peace or chaos it brings.

The difference between scarcity and stewardship is not in your income. It is in your perspective. Two people can make the same amount of money and live completely different financial lives. One lives in constant tension, saving and spending from fear, always worried about what might happen next. The other feels calm, intentional, and grounded. Their situation is not perfect, but it is peaceful. The only difference between them is what they believe.

I used to live in scarcity without knowing it. I told myself I was being responsible, but every decision came from fear. I saved not because I wanted to build something, but because I was terrified of losing everything. I worked not because I loved what I did, but because slowing down felt dangerous. Every choice was driven by the belief that if I stopped moving, everything would fall apart.

That is the exhausting part about scarcity. It never lets you rest. You can be doing everything right and still feel like you are one mistake away from disaster. You start to confuse exhaustion with achievement. You think the anxiety means you are succeeding, when really, it means you are surviving.

Stewardship, on the other hand, feels steady. It is not about hoarding or indulging. It is about balance. It begins with the belief that what you already have is enough to manage well. You do not have to be rich to be a good steward. You only have to care about what has been entrusted to you.

When you think like a steward, you stop asking, "What if I lose it?" and start asking, "How can I grow it?" You stop reacting to fear and start responding with intention. You begin to see every dollar as a decision, and every decision as a reflection of your values. Money stops being emotional and starts being directional.

The shift from scarcity to stewardship is not sudden. It happens slowly, through small acts of awareness. It begins when you stop making choices from panic and start making them from purpose. It shows up when you pause before a purchase, not to judge yourself, but to ask what that choice is doing for your future. It deepens when you start viewing money as something you manage, not something that manages you.

Scarcity makes you believe that stability only comes from accumulation. Stewardship teaches you that stability comes from order. You can have a small amount of money and still live peacefully if you manage it with care. You can have a large amount of money and still feel desperate if you manage it with fear. The peace is not in the number. It is in the mindset.

That realization changes everything. Once you start viewing money through the lens of stewardship, you stop trying to control it and start trying to direct it. You make decisions not to protect yourself from loss, but to prepare yourself for growth. You begin to give with joy, because you no longer see generosity as depletion. You start saving because you value preparation more than panic. You start investing because you believe in your ability to handle risk with wisdom.

Stewardship is not about perfection. It is about presence. It is the habit of paying attention to your money, not from fear but from respect. When you live this way, you begin to see that money has always been trying to teach you something about yourself. It reflects your discipline, your patience, your trust, and your priorities. When you manage it with care, you become more peaceful not just financially, but emotionally.

I used to believe that money revealed character only when you had a lot of it. Now I see that it reveals character in every stage. The way you handle a hundred dollars is a preview of how you will handle ten thousand. The way you plan for the future when things are tight shows the kind of person you will be when things are abundant.

That is why stewardship is so powerful. It does not depend on circumstance. It is an attitude that can be practiced in any season. It can begin with a single paycheck or a single decision to take ownership of what you already have.

When you live in scarcity, you hold on tightly because you believe there will never be enough. When you live in stewardship, you hold on wisely because you believe there will always be purpose. Scarcity drains your peace. Stewardship restores it. Scarcity makes you frantic. Stewardship makes you focused.

The more you practice stewardship, the less power money has over your emotions. You begin to find peace in the process itself. The same numbers that once made you anxious start to feel like tools you can use. You still care about growth and security, but now they come from clarity instead of fear.

That is the heart of showing up financially. It is not about chasing wealth or living in worry. It is about learning to manage what you have with care, confidence, and gratitude. It is about choosing order over panic and purpose over pressure.

The shift will not always feel natural. Scarcity is stubborn. It will try to whisper that you are falling behind, that you are foolish for feeling calm, that something must be wrong if everything feels stable. When those thoughts appear, remember that peace does not mean passivity. It means mastery. It means you are finally in control of what used to control you.

Stewardship is what turns money from a master into a servant. It gives you authority over your resources, not by increasing them, but by understanding them. It transforms the way you think about earning, spending, saving, and giving.

When you live with that mindset, you no longer chase freedom through numbers. You build it through discipline. You find peace not in the amount you possess, but in the awareness that you are managing it well.

That is how scarcity loses its grip. It cannot survive in the presence of stewardship. One feeds fear. The other builds peace.

And once you learn to live as a steward, you realize that money has finally taken its proper place in your life. It is no longer the source of your stress. It has become the expression of your strength.

SIX

Facing the Numbers Without Fear

Most people spend their lives avoiding the truth about their money. Not because they are lazy or careless, but because they are afraid of what the truth might show. They would rather live with the quiet stress of not knowing than face the sharp discomfort of looking.

I know that feeling. I have opened my bank account and held my breath. I have seen a balance that made my stomach drop and immediately closed the screen, telling myself I would deal with it later. Later rarely came. What did come was more stress, more avoidance, and more shame.

Avoidance feels safe at first, but it always turns into anxiety. The longer you wait to look, the heavier it becomes. Every unopened bill starts to carry the weight of failure. Every unreviewed statement becomes proof that you are behind. But here is the truth. The fear you feel about your finances is almost never about the numbers themselves. It is about the story you tell yourself about what those numbers mean.

Most people believe that if they face their finances, they will confirm their worst fears. They think the numbers will tell them they have failed, that they are irresponsible, that they are not capable. But when you finally gather the courage to look, you usually discover something much more ordinary. You are not bad with money. You are just disconnected from it.

Money does not respond to avoidance. It responds to attention. It is neutral until you give it direction. That means you can change its path, but not until you know where it currently stands.

When you face your numbers honestly,
something surprising happens. The fear begins
to fade. The power you thought the numbers
held starts to shrink because information
replaces imagination. The unknown is always
scarier than the truth. Once you know the truth,
even if it is not pretty, you can work with it.

Clarity is not cruel. It is kind. It gives you back
the power to act.

Facing your numbers is not about judging
yourself. It is about knowing yourself. It is a
moment of maturity, not punishment. When you
finally sit down and see everything clearly, you
stop guessing. You stop telling yourself vague
stories about how things might be and start
seeing what actually is.

That single act of honesty is the moment most
people start to change. Because once you see it,
you can never go back to pretending.

You do not need fancy spreadsheets or complex
systems to begin. You only need honesty. Take a
quiet hour and gather everything you can. The
goal is not to feel overwhelmed. The goal is to
see the whole picture. You might find that
things are not as bad as you imagined. You

might also find that they are worse. Either way, now you know, and knowing gives you options.

When you stop running from your numbers, you start to see that money is not emotional. It only mirrors your habits. The emotion comes from what those habits mean to you. If you see spending where you meant to save, that does not make you weak. It makes you human. If you see debt where you wanted progress, that does not make you a failure. It means you have been living without clarity.

Understanding replaces shame. Once you know where you stand, you can build a plan that fits who you are. You can adjust, refine, and grow. It will not happen overnight, but the peace begins immediately. The stress you have been carrying starts to lift because uncertainty is heavier than any number could ever be.

I remember the first time I sat down and calculated everything honestly. I expected devastation. What I found was relief. For the first time, I knew exactly where I stood. I could see the problem clearly. It was not easy, but it was simple. I had been fighting shadows, and the moment I turned the light on, they disappeared.

The truth is that facing your numbers is an act of self-respect. It is saying to yourself, "I am capable of handling what I have created." It is refusing to stay blind to the consequences of your choices, but also refusing to be defined by them. You cannot grow from what you will not see. You cannot fix what you will not face.

Once you begin, it gets easier. The first look is the hardest. After that, you start to find calm in the clarity. You begin to check your accounts not out of panic but out of purpose. You start to plan your spending instead of reacting to it. You notice patterns, make small adjustments, and watch as the numbers slowly start to move in your favor. Progress replaces panic. Awareness replaces avoidance.

You will also notice how your emotions shift. The shame you once felt begins to fade. You no longer feel like your finances are happening to you. You begin to feel like you are in charge of them. That sense of control creates momentum. It makes you more intentional, more thoughtful, and more confident.

People often think financial peace comes from wealth. It does not. It comes from awareness. Wealth without awareness creates stress just as easily as struggle does. The size of your income matters far less than your understanding of it. Peace comes from knowing your numbers and trusting yourself to manage them.

Facing the truth is always the first step to freedom. When you finally stop hiding from your financial reality, you start creating a new one. You move from confusion to clarity, from reaction to intention. You become someone who leads your money rather than someone who fears it.

And as strange as it sounds, that moment of honesty will bring more relief than any paycheck ever could. Because you will know that you are no longer pretending. You are no longer letting the unknown rule your thoughts. You have faced the numbers, and they did not destroy you. They empowered you.

That is the quiet turning point in every financial story. The moment you stop fearing the truth and start using it. The moment you realize that the math is not the enemy. It is the map. It will show you exactly where you are and exactly how to get where you want to go.

Showing up financially starts with that single act of courage. It starts the day you decide to look. Because until you face your numbers, you cannot face your future.

And once you do, you will realize that the hardest part was never the money itself. It was the fear.

Now that you have faced it, the fear no longer has a place to hide.

SEVEN

Pay Yourself First

If you have ever worked hard week after week only to end up wondering where it all went, you are not alone. You look at your account, remember the hours you gave, and feel a quiet sense of frustration. You did everything right, yet somehow there is nothing left to show for it. It is easy to believe the problem is the size of your paycheck. But the deeper truth is that the problem is often the order of your priorities.

For most people, money leaves their hands before they ever get a chance to direct it. The bills, the groceries, the subscriptions, the things that "just come out." And by the time you think about saving, there is nothing left. That pattern feels normal, but it quietly trains you to put your future last.

Paying yourself first is how you reverse that story. It is not a trick or a slogan. It is a way of treating yourself with respect. It says that the person doing the work deserves to benefit from the work. It means you value your time and effort enough to protect part of it.

Most of us grew up thinking that discipline meant sacrifice. We believed that saving meant missing out. But paying yourself first is not about restriction. It is about recognition. It is about finally acknowledging that your effort has value beyond today.

This principle works because it connects money to identity. Every time you pay yourself first, you are reinforcing who you are becoming. You are telling yourself that you can be trusted with responsibility. You are saying, "I follow through." That is how financial confidence begins.

In the beginning, it will not feel easy. The first few paychecks might feel tighter. You will want to skip a transfer or tell yourself that next month will be better. But if you stick with it, something quiet begins to change. You start to see saving as a habit, not a hope. You start to feel proud instead of pressured.

When I first committed to this, I started with an amount so small it almost felt pointless. But that small amount represented something bigger. It represented consistency. Within a few months, the habit took root. I stopped debating with myself about whether to save and simply expected it to happen. That is when I realized that saving is less about money and more about momentum.

The magic of paying yourself first is that it builds self-respect through repetition. Each time you save, you remind yourself that your work means something. Each deposit becomes a small act of dignity. You are no longer hoping there will be leftovers. You are guaranteeing that there will be something waiting for you tomorrow.

This is how habits reshape identity. When you choose to act like someone who values their future, you start to believe it. That belief then changes how you spend, how you plan, and how you see yourself.

The habit also changes how you handle setbacks. When life happens, and it will, the person who pays themselves first already has a cushion. They have room to breathe. They can recover without panic because they have built margin into their life. That margin is not just financial. It is emotional. It gives you space to make calm decisions instead of desperate ones.

You do not need to start big. You only need to start before you feel ready. The amount is less important than the order. The moment the money arrives, you send a portion to yourself. You can automate it if you like, but even doing it manually for the first few months helps the pattern take hold. Each time you do, you are strengthening the link between intention and action.

Think about what this teaches your mind. Every time you save, you delay gratification. You choose long-term peace over short-term relief. You build patience, and patience always pays interest in peace. Over time, you stop fighting with yourself. The habit becomes natural, and that natural rhythm brings freedom.

The deeper reason this works is because it heals a quiet wound. Many people grew up in households where money was scarce or unpredictable. They learned early to survive each week rather than plan for the next one. Paying yourself first interrupts that generational story. It tells your nervous system,

"We are safe now." It shows that you are no longer living in reaction but in responsibility.

The more consistent you become, the more trust you build with yourself. You start to believe that you can handle the future. That belief is what creates confidence. True financial peace does not come from numbers. It comes from the self-trust you feel when you know you will follow through.

As that confidence grows, you begin to see the ripple effects. You make better decisions because you feel grounded. You are less impulsive because you no longer need instant comfort. You stop chasing temporary rewards because you have already built a system that provides lasting ones. The respect you give your money reflects the respect you give yourself.

There will still be moments when you slip. You will have months when saving feels impossible. But the habit is not about perfection. It is about persistence. When you get off track, start again immediately. Each restart strengthens the habit even more.

Over time, the results compound quietly. The numbers grow, yes, but something greater grows with them. You begin to feel lighter. You look at your account and realize that you are not just saving money. You are saving evidence that you are capable. You are proving that discipline is not punishment. It is peace in motion.

The people who struggle most with money are often the ones who never learned to value their own labor. They work hard but never keep any part of what they earn. Paying yourself first fixes that imbalance. It teaches you that you are worthy of the same care you give to everyone else.

When you make this a lifelong habit, you stop surviving your finances and start leading them. You stop wondering where the money went because you already told it where to go. You stop hoping for stability because you are actively creating it.

This is not greed. It is stewardship. It is the practical side of self-respect. You are not saving to escape responsibility. You are saving to sustain it.

And when you look back months or years from now, you will realize that this single habit changed more than your balance. It changed your belief. It taught you that your effort deserves a return, and that peace is not something you find later. It is something you build every time you choose yourself with purpose.

Paying yourself first is not about being rich. It is about being ready. It is about knowing that the future version of you will look back with gratitude and say, "You kept your promise."

That is the real reward. Not just the savings you built, but the self-respect you built with it.

EIGHT

The Power of Automation

Once you begin paying yourself first, the next step is learning how to make that habit automatic. Discipline builds momentum, but automation protects it.

Most people know what they should do with their money. They know they should save, invest, pay down debt, and stay on top of bills. The problem is not knowledge. The problem is consistency. Life gets busy. Decisions pile up. One forgotten transfer turns into a missed opportunity, and before you realize it, the habit you worked hard to build begins to slip.

Automation is how you protect yourself from that drift. It takes the most important financial decisions out of the daily noise and locks them into place. Once you set it up, your money begins to move with quiet purpose even when you are not thinking about it. It becomes a system that serves you instead of one that depends on your willpower.

There was a time when I tried to manage everything manually. I told myself that staying involved meant staying responsible. I would move money between accounts, schedule reminders, and promise myself that next month I would be more organized. It worked for a while, until it didn't. The moment life got busy, my best intentions fell apart. I realized that responsibility is not about handling everything yourself. It is about building systems that can handle it with you.

Automation is one of the simplest ways to do that. When your savings, bills, and investments happen automatically, you no longer rely on memory or mood. You remove emotion from the process. The money moves whether you feel motivated or distracted. You create a rhythm that supports you even on the days when you are tired or overwhelmed.

The beauty of automation is that it turns good choices into defaults. Instead of fighting to make the right decision over and over, you make it once. You decide the amount, the timing, and the destination, and then you let the system run. Each paycheck, a portion goes exactly where it should. You begin to live in alignment with your goals without the constant effort of remembering them.

This is not about giving up control. It is about designing control in advance. You are still the one directing your money. You are simply setting the path ahead of time so that each dollar knows where to go before it ever lands in your account. Automation is the practical expression of stewardship. It shows that you trust yourself enough to plan ahead.

At first, setting it up can feel intimidating. You might worry about committing to transfers before you know how the month will unfold. But that small discomfort is worth it. It forces you to plan instead of react. It makes you think ahead and prepare for what matters most. And once it is in place, it becomes one of the most peaceful parts of your financial life.

When your savings happen automatically, you stop waiting for leftover money to appear. You build consistency without constant effort. When your bills are paid automatically, you remove the anxiety of deadlines and late fees. When your investments grow automatically, you turn time into your partner instead of your enemy. Every automated step is a quiet declaration that your finances are moving forward, even when you are not watching.

Automation also builds confidence. Each time you see those transfers happen on schedule, you are reminded that you are capable of managing your life with order. That sense of control changes the way you view money. It no longer feels chaotic. It feels structured and predictable. Even when things get tight, you have a clear understanding of where everything stands.

I used to think that automation was only for people who had a lot of money. I assumed that until I had more, I needed to stay hands-on. What I eventually learned was that automation is what helps you build more. It removes the friction that makes saving difficult. It frees up mental energy so you can focus on bigger goals instead of daily maintenance. It keeps you moving forward quietly, without the emotional weight that comes from managing every detail.

The key to automation is starting small but being consistent. You do not have to overhaul everything at once. Begin with one thing. Maybe it is your savings transfer. Maybe it is your most important bill. Let that one process run smoothly before adding the next. Over time, your system will grow naturally. It will feel less like management and more like flow.

Once your financial life begins to run on these systems, you notice something powerful. You start spending less energy on worry. The same actions that once felt heavy begin to feel effortless. You begin to realize that success is not about intensity. It is about consistency.

Automation does not remove responsibility. It amplifies it. It keeps you accountable even when your motivation fades. It ensures that your best intentions do not get buried under everyday chaos. It is the bridge between what you know you should do and what you actually do.

There is also an emotional freedom that comes with this structure. When you know that your essentials are handled, you can be more present in your life. You can enjoy moments without the background hum of financial stress. You can focus on growth, creativity, or family instead of remembering due dates. You create a sense of calm that no paycheck alone can buy.

At its core, automation is about trust. You are teaching yourself that you can build systems that work. You are proving that discipline does not have to be constant effort. It can be designed into your life. Each automated action becomes a vote for the person you want to be. It says, "I am someone who follows through, even when I am busy."

The more you trust that system, the more confident you become in your ability to lead your finances. You stop fearing mistakes because your foundation is secure. You stop chasing stability because you have already built it. You begin to understand that peace is not found in perfection, but in structure.

Automation is quiet, but it is powerful. It does not need attention or applause. It simply works in the background, building strength while you live your life. It is one of the most practical forms of wisdom there is. It protects your progress and keeps you moving forward long after motivation fades.

Showing up financially is not about doing everything manually or proving your discipline through struggle. It is about creating order that supports you. Automation is that order. It is the invisible system that keeps your life aligned with your values.

When you build that kind of structure, you begin to experience what real financial peace feels like. It is not excitement. It is not luck. It is quiet confidence. The kind that comes from knowing that your money is working for you, even when you are not watching.

That is the power of automation. It turns your best intentions into your daily reality. And once you experience that, you will never want to go back.

NINE

Breaking the Time-for-Money Trade

Most people live their entire lives trapped in a quiet exchange. They trade hours for income, believing that the more time they give, the more secure they will become. It feels logical, even responsible. You work, you earn, you rest, you repeat. It is the rhythm society teaches you to follow. The problem is that this rhythm never ends. You can work harder, longer, and better, but as long as your income depends entirely on your effort, your freedom will always be limited.

Trading time for money is not a flaw. It is how most of us begin. Every job, every business, every career starts with effort. The problem is when effort becomes the ceiling instead of the foundation. If your income stops the moment you do, then what you really have is not stability. It is dependency.

This realization often feels uncomfortable. You start to see that no matter how good you are at what you do, there will always be a limit to how much you can earn. You only have so many hours, so much energy, and so many years to give. That is the invisible cost of the time-for-money trap. It looks safe, but it quietly steals your future.

I learned this lesson the hard way. For years, I thought that being busy meant being successful. I worked long hours, took on extra projects, and told myself I was building something meaningful. In reality, I was building a cage. I had convinced myself that working harder was the only path to peace, but all it gave me was exhaustion. I was surviving through effort, not thriving through design.

Breaking the time-for-money trade does not mean quitting your job or abandoning responsibility. It means changing the way you think about value. Your worth is not measured by how many hours you give, but by how effectively you use them. Freedom begins when you start creating things that continue to produce value even when you are not there.

That is what separates workers from builders. Workers give time. Builders create systems. Both matter, but only one leads to freedom.

If you are in a traditional job, this concept still applies. You might not control your paycheck completely, but you can control what you build with it. You can use your income to invest, to create, or to develop skills that multiply your earning potential. You can start small side projects that generate residual income. You can pay down debt and free up time that used to belong to creditors. Every action that reduces dependency on constant labor is a step toward freedom.

When you begin to see time as your most valuable asset, you start spending it differently. You begin asking better questions. Instead of asking, "How can I make more money?" you start asking, "How can I make money work without me?" That single shift in thinking changes everything. It moves you from effort to efficiency. From labor to leverage.

Leverage is the key. It is what allows your effort to expand beyond your hours. You can create leverage through knowledge, through people, through systems, or through assets. You can write something once that earns forever. You can design a process that runs without constant supervision. You can invest in something that grows quietly in the background. The form does not matter. The principle does.

The principle is this: your goal is not to stop working. Your goal is to make sure your work keeps working even when you are not.

When you understand that, you start treating your time like currency. You stop spending it carelessly and start investing it wisely. Every skill you learn, every system you build, every decision you automate becomes a form of compound interest on your life.

This shift is not about greed or laziness. It is about stewardship. It is about recognizing that you are not meant to spend your entire life earning just enough to get by. You are meant to build something that outlives your effort.

At first, this can feel unrealistic. You might think, "That is easy for someone else, but I do

not have the freedom to do that." The truth is,
you already have more freedom than you think.
The moment you decide to use part of your time
for creation instead of reaction, you begin to
reclaim your power. You do not need to overhaul
your life in a single week. You start by
protecting small pockets of time and using them
with intention.

Maybe that time goes toward learning a skill
that opens new doors. Maybe it goes toward
setting up an automated income stream, like a
digital product, an investment account, or a
small business that runs part-time. Maybe it
simply goes toward organizing your finances so
your future self can breathe easier. The
specifics will look different for everyone, but
the goal is the same. You are shifting from
working for money to working with it.

Once you begin this process, something changes
inside you. You stop seeing yourself as an
employee of your finances and start seeing
yourself as the leader of them. You become
more strategic, more creative, and more
confident. You begin to realize that time, not
money, is the real measure of wealth.

Money without time is just a nicer form of
captivity. True financial peace is not having

more. It is having control over when and how you work. It is waking up and knowing that your life is no longer dictated entirely by the clock.

Building that kind of freedom takes time, but it starts with a simple mindset: every hour you give to something should buy you back more hours in the future. That is the test of whether something is building your future or draining it.

When you live this way, your days feel different. You still work hard, but it feels purposeful. You still earn, but you earn with intention. You are not just maintaining. You are multiplying. You are building momentum that keeps growing even when you are not watching.

That is how freedom is built quietly, day by day. It is not sudden. It is steady. It comes from small shifts that compound over time. You stop living for the weekend and start designing a life that does not need escape.

Breaking the time-for-money trade is not about rejecting work. It is about redeeming it. It is about using your energy to build something lasting instead of something that disappears every two weeks with your paycheck.

When you begin to think this way, you start showing up differently in every part of your financial life. You plan with purpose. You spend with vision. You stop settling for survival and start aiming for freedom.

Because the truth is, time will always be your most valuable currency. Once it is spent, you cannot earn it back. But when you learn how to make money work for you, you start buying time instead of losing it.

That is when you realize what real wealth feels like. It is not in the amount you earn. It is in the amount of life you get to live.

TEN

The Compounding Advantage

Time can be your greatest ally or your most expensive enemy. It depends on how you use it.

Most people underestimate the quiet power of time. They think progress comes from big moves, from sudden changes or lucky breaks. But real growth almost never happens that way. The truth is, most financial success is not about brilliance or timing. It is about consistency. It is about doing the right thing long enough for time to multiply the results. That is the compounding advantage.

Compounding is what happens when your effort, your money, or your discipline begins to earn its own return. It is growth that builds on itself, quietly, day after day. It is not glamorous. It is not fast. But it is unstoppable once it starts.

The same principle applies whether you are talking about investing, saving, or self-improvement. The small, boring, consistent actions that seem insignificant in the moment are the ones that build strength over time. The problem is that most people never stay consistent long enough to see that growth. They give up just before the curve starts to bend in their favor.

Compounding rewards patience, not perfection. It does not care about how much you start with. It cares about how long you stay with it. Every day, every dollar, every decision adds another layer to what you are building.

When I first started saving, the results were almost invisible. The balance grew slowly, a few dollars at a time. It was easy to wonder if it even mattered. But then something shifted. As time passed, those small amounts began to build momentum. The progress became visible. It was like watching a snowball roll downhill, gathering speed and weight with every turn. The same thing happens with money, discipline, and peace. The reward begins slowly, but it never stops once it starts.

The compounding advantage is not limited to investments or savings accounts. It exists in every habit you form. When you choose to make one wise financial decision, you do not just help yourself today. You make tomorrow easier. When you keep showing up, your future starts to work for you instead of against you.

You can see this principle in almost every part of life. The person who reads a few pages a day becomes more knowledgeable than the person who crams once a year. The person who walks every morning stays healthier than the person who tries a new workout once a month. The person who saves a small percentage of every paycheck ends up wealthier than the one who waits for the perfect time to start. The compounding advantage rewards consistency.

Financially, this is how you make time your partner. You give your money a job and let it work quietly in the background. The earlier you start, the more powerful it becomes. The same dollar saved today can grow into many times its value in the future, not because you added more, but because you gave it time.

Most people overestimate what they can do in a year and underestimate what they can do in ten. They want immediate results, but compounding does not respond to impatience. It rewards the steady. It favors the person who plants early and keeps watering even when there is nothing to see.

The same principle applies emotionally. When you build a habit of saving, giving, or investing, you are not just growing wealth. You are growing confidence. Each time you follow through, you reinforce the belief that you are capable of consistency. That belief compounds too. It spills into other areas of your life. You become more patient, more focused, and more secure.

I remember meeting someone who had started saving a small amount from their first job. It was almost nothing at the time, just enough to feel responsible. Twenty years later, that habit had built a foundation that no sudden stroke of luck could have matched. They were not wealthy because they were brilliant. They were free because they were consistent.

That is what the compounding advantage gives you. Freedom. It does not just grow your money. It grows your time, your confidence, and your options. It gives you breathing room. It turns patience into power.

But here is the part most people miss. Compounding works both ways. It does not only multiply good choices. It also multiplies neglect. The same way small deposits build wealth, small delays build debt. A missed payment becomes two. A small expense becomes a habit. A few months of inaction become years of lost progress. Time is neutral. It multiplies whatever you give it.

That is why awareness matters so much. You cannot stop time, but you can decide what it is working on. You can feed it the right actions. You can align it with your goals. You can make sure that every day is adding to your future instead of taking from it.

There will always be moments when it feels like progress is too slow. You might look at your balance or your goals and think, "This is not working." That is the test. Compounding rewards the ones who keep going anyway. It demands trust. It asks you to believe that even when growth is invisible, it is still happening.

One day, the results appear all at once. The slow becomes sudden. The invisible becomes obvious. And you realize that what felt small was never wasted. It was building strength the whole time.

That is why compounding is not just a financial principle. It is a mindset. It teaches you that steady effort will always outperform frantic action. It reminds you that peace grows the same way as wealth, slowly and steadily. It shows you that the real advantage in life does not come from doing everything fast. It comes from doing the right things long enough.

You do not have to master the markets or make perfect choices to benefit from this. You only have to start and stay. The habit itself is the win. Every week that you keep the system running, every month that you stay consistent, you are letting time work for you instead of against you.

Eventually, you stop worrying about quick results. You begin to trust the process. You find comfort in knowing that time is now on your side. Each day you keep going, your life builds quiet strength.

The compounding advantage is not magic. It is math, multiplied by patience. It is how small actions become freedom. It is how ordinary people build extraordinary peace.

When you look back years from now, you will not remember the exact moment things turned around. You will realize that it was never one moment. It was all of them. The quiet decisions. The simple habits. The steady faith that what you were building was worth it.

That is the beauty of compounding. It rewards those who show up.

Because time, when used wisely, always pays interest in peace.

ELEVEN

Financial Freedom Math

For most of your life, you have probably been
told that financial success means having more.
More income, more savings, more growth, more
everything. It is a simple idea, but it creates an
endless chase. Because no matter how much
"more" you have, someone else will always have
a little extra. There will always be a higher
number, a bigger goal, a new comparison
waiting just ahead.

That is why so many people who earn well still
feel anxious. They do not know what "enough"
looks like. They measure success by expansion
instead of freedom. They build bigger houses,

drive newer cars, and upgrade everything around them, but they rarely upgrade their peace. They have mastered income but not contentment.

Financial freedom does not come from more. It comes from clarity. It comes from knowing your number.

Your number is the point where your life runs smoothly without pressure. It is the point where your bills are paid, your savings are consistent, and your mind is quiet. It is the point where money supports your values instead of competing with them. It looks different for everyone, but the purpose is always the same. To define "enough" before the world convinces you to keep chasing.

I did not always think this way. For years, I assumed that freedom meant abundance. I thought the more I earned, the freer I would feel. But every time my income grew, my expenses followed. Each milestone simply raised the standard. What I called progress was really inflation disguised as success. I had more money, but I did not have more peace.

The truth hit me one night when I realized I was
earning well but sleeping poorly. I was still
worried. Still grinding. Still reacting to the
same stress in a different bracket. That was
when I began to ask a different question.
Instead of "How do I make more?" I started
asking, "How much is enough?"

That question changed everything. It forced me
to get honest about what I actually needed to
live a life that felt full. Not impressive, but
peaceful. Not showy, but stable. It made me
confront how much of my effort was driven by
ego instead of purpose.

When you do this work yourself, you begin to
realize that freedom is mathematical. It is not
abstract. It can be measured. It can be planned.
It can be built.

Start by looking at the essentials that make your
life function. The roof, the food, the bills, the
transportation, the things that truly matter. Add
to that the savings, the giving, the experiences
that bring you joy. When you know that number,
you stop chasing vague ideas of wealth and start
pursuing something real. You stop working
without direction and start building with
precision.

This is what I call financial freedom math. It is simple addition and subtraction, but with purpose behind it. It gives you a target. It turns dreams into numbers and numbers into plans.

When you know your number, decisions become easier. You can say yes and no with confidence. You can separate what adds value from what only adds noise. You stop feeling guilty for not doing more and start feeling grateful for what you already have.

The interesting part is that your number is usually smaller than you think. Most people overestimate how much it takes to live freely. They assume that peace requires luxury, when in reality, peace only requires alignment. If your lifestyle reflects your values, you can feel rich long before the balance sheet says so.

The math of freedom is not about maximizing earnings. It is about minimizing dependency. It is about building a life that costs less than you make and feels fuller than it looks. It is about creating systems that support you instead of draining you. When your income covers your needs, supports your goals, and leaves space for generosity and rest, you are already wealthy. You may not feel that way at first, but wealth is not just measured in dollars. It is measured in time, in calm, and in choice.

Financial freedom math also teaches you responsibility. Once you know your number, you realize that every decision has impact. Every subscription, every loan, every impulse purchase either moves you closer to or further from that peace. You begin to see your money as a map of your values. The things that matter rise to the surface. The things that do not start to fade.

I once worked with someone who earned far more than they ever thought possible, yet they felt trapped. Every dollar was already spoken for. Their life looked successful from the outside, but the inside was full of pressure. We sat down and defined their number, their real number, the one that covered everything important without all the excess. They were shocked by how attainable it was. The moment they realized it, they said something I will never forget: "I've been running this hard for years, and I passed freedom a long time ago without even seeing it."

That is what happens to most people. They pass freedom because they never stopped to define it.

When you know your number, you reclaim direction. You start working on purpose. You begin to see that you do not have to escape your life to enjoy it. You simply need to design it intentionally.

This is not about settling. It is about mastering. Once you reach your freedom number, your money is no longer your master. You are free to keep building, giving, or growing, but not because you need to. Because you want to. That difference is everything. It turns striving into stewardship. It transforms your financial goals from survival into expression.

The math of freedom is not complicated. It is honest. It is a tool for clarity. It reminds you that peace cannot be borrowed, and contentment cannot be bought. Both are built when you know what you actually need and have the discipline to live inside it.

The most powerful moment in any financial journey is when you realize that freedom is closer than you thought. It is not waiting on a raise or a miracle. It is waiting on awareness.

When you finally define what enough looks like, you can stop running. You can stop measuring success by other people's standards. You can build a life that fits you instead of one that exhausts you.

Financial freedom math gives you permission to rest. It reminds you that abundance is not just about accumulation. It is about alignment. It is about understanding that the goal is not to have it all. The goal is to have enough and to live fully within it.

When you reach that point, money becomes simple again. It goes back to being a tool, not a test. It becomes something that supports your peace instead of threatening it.

That is what it means to be free. Not the absence of responsibility, but the presence of clarity. You finally know what you are working toward, and you can feel good about stopping when you get there.

Because real success is not how far you go. It is how well you live once you arrive.

TWELVE

Making Money Work for You

There comes a point in every financial journey when you realize that working harder is no longer the answer. You have already given your time, your effort, your late nights. You are not lazy, and you are not failing. You have simply reached the limit of what one person can do alone.

That is where the next level begins. Real financial growth is not about effort. It is about structure. It is about learning how to make money work while you rest, live, and focus on what matters most.

Most people never make that shift. They spend their whole lives earning and spending, trapped in the same loop. They tell themselves that if they just make a little more, everything will finally feel stable. But more income without intention only makes the pattern spin faster. The only way out is to change the relationship. You stop working for money and start leading it.

Money is a tool, and like any tool, it performs best with direction. When you give it purpose, it multiplies what you care about. When you leave it unmanaged, it works for someone else.

Think about how most people treat their income. It comes in, it goes out, and they hope something good happens in between. But money is not supposed to drift. It needs a job. Every dollar should have a task that supports your larger goals. Some should work for safety, some for growth, and some for generosity. When each one knows where to go, you are no longer reacting to your finances. You are directing them.

Making money work for you starts with structure. If you built the habit of paying yourself first, you already know how to create consistency. Now you extend that mindset further. You turn habits into systems. Systems remove emotion. They protect progress when life gets busy or stressful.

Automation is the simplest form of leverage. When your money moves automatically toward your goals, you do not have to rely on discipline alone. Your systems do the heavy lifting. Your savings grow. Your investments compound. Your bills are handled. The machine runs even when you are tired. That is not control. That is wisdom.

The truth is that automation is not about convenience. It is about peace. It removes the daily noise so you can think clearly. It gives you the mental space to focus on the future instead of fighting fires. Every process you automate buys back time, and time is the most valuable currency you have.

This is how wealth begins — not with luck or windfalls, but with repeatable systems that protect your energy. When money starts working in the background, you finally have room to live in the foreground.

As your systems grow, you will start to see leverage differently. You realize that your income is not just what you earn from your job.

It is what your systems produce while you are living your life. Investments, savings, and even small streams of passive income become quiet employees. They work without asking for rest.

You do not have to be an expert investor or a business owner to make this happen. You simply have to think like a leader. Leaders give direction. They design systems that reflect their values. They measure progress, make adjustments, and stay patient. That same mindset works with money.

Think of yourself as the manager of your financial team. Your dollars are the employees. Each one has a role to play. If you do not assign those roles, they wander. They drift toward distractions. But when you lead them with purpose, they build something meaningful.

That is what separates people who feel constant pressure from those who feel steady. Both groups work hard. The difference is that one leads their money and the other chases it.

Making money work for you does not mean chasing quick returns or complex strategies. It means building systems that align with your values and goals. It means designing a flow where your income supports your peace instead of disturbing it.

There will still be seasons where things tighten. But when your systems are in place, those seasons do not break you. They simply slow you down for a while. Your foundation remains solid because it does not depend on your energy alone.

This shift also changes how you view success. You stop measuring progress by how exhausted you are. You start measuring it by how well your systems run without you. True freedom is when your finances keep growing even when you are not thinking about them.

It takes patience to reach that point. It will not happen overnight. But each small adjustment compounds. Each time you delegate another financial task to a system, you free yourself to think more strategically. You begin to live less like an employee of your money and more like its leader.

Eventually, the peace you feel from these systems will spill into every other area of your life. You will have more attention for your relationships, your health, and your purpose because your financial life no longer consumes your energy. You will feel supported, not stretched.

That is what it truly means to make money work for you. It is not just about earning interest or creating passive income. It is about designing your life so that your money supports your wellbeing instead of stealing it. It is about building processes that serve your priorities without constant supervision.

When that shift happens, something subtle but powerful changes inside you. You stop waking up with financial tension in the back of your mind. You stop checking balances in fear. You stop feeling like life is always on the edge of falling apart. You begin to trust your systems. You begin to trust yourself.

This is the highest form of stewardship — not reacting, but designing. Not chasing, but leading. Not working endlessly for peace, but building peace that works endlessly for you.

Making money work for you is not about control. It is about partnership. It is the point where your effort and your systems meet and start multiplying together.

And that is where financial freedom quietly begins to grow.

THIRTEEN

Smart Debt, Dumb Debt

Debt is one of those topics that instantly divides people. Some treat it like a weapon. Others treat it like a curse. A few pretend it doesn't exist. But the truth is, debt is none of those things by itself. It is not good or bad. It is simply a tool. The problem is how it gets used.

Money has a language, and debt speaks it fluently. It can say "freedom" or "bondage" depending on who is holding it and why. The difference between smart debt and dumb debt is not in the interest rate. It is in the intention.

Dumb debt is the kind that controls you. It grows from reaction, impulse, or emotion. It happens when you borrow to fill a void or to buy peace you haven't yet earned. Dumb debt promises relief but delivers pressure. It gives you the illusion of progress while quietly chaining you to the past.

Smart debt, on the other hand, is debt with a purpose. It is taken strategically, with a clear plan and a specific end in mind. It creates opportunity, not anxiety. It builds something that will eventually pay you back, directly or indirectly. It moves you closer to freedom, not further into obligation.

The truth is that debt itself does not ruin lives. Confusion does. Most people get into trouble not because they borrowed, but because they borrowed without clarity. They didn't understand the real cost of their decision. They looked at the monthly payment and not the long-term consequence. They said yes to a feeling and not to a plan.

I have been there. I have justified purchases that felt responsible in the moment, only to realize later that they came from pressure, not purpose. The weight that followed was heavier than the object I bought. What I learned through that experience is that every loan, every credit card, every payment is a relationship. And like any relationship, it will either support you or drain you.

Dumb debt feels urgent. It always tells you that you need it right now. It thrives on impulse. It is emotional and impatient. It feeds off insecurity. It convinces you that buying something will fill a gap that discipline could have fixed. It offers short-term comfort at the cost of long-term peace.

Smart debt feels patient. It takes time to understand. It has a clear reason for existing and a defined way out. It might be a business loan that generates income, a mortgage that builds equity, or an education that increases earning potential. It costs something, but it produces something greater in return.

The goal is not to eliminate all debt from your life forever. The goal is to understand it so well that it never surprises you. You can use debt strategically without becoming dependent on it. You can borrow with wisdom and repay with peace.

When you look at your finances, ask yourself what every debt represents. Does it reflect fear or faith? Does it build the life you want or maintain the one you feel stuck in? These questions matter because debt has energy. It carries emotion. It shapes how you feel about your future.

For some people, debt is a constant source of guilt. They look at their balances and feel ashamed, as if the numbers define their worth. But shame never pays a bill. It only keeps you frozen. What actually changes your situation is ownership. The moment you stop hiding from your debt and start managing it, the weight begins to lift. You cannot outwork something you refuse to face.

Once you have faced it, the strategy becomes simple. You decide what to keep and what to clear. You begin to rebuild trust with yourself through consistency. Each payment becomes a step toward freedom instead of a reminder of failure. The progress might be slow, but it is steady. And steady progress is how every mountain gets climbed.

There is also an emotional shift that happens when you start managing debt intentionally. You stop viewing payments as punishment and start seeing them as progress. You stop feeling like a victim and start acting like a leader. You begin to realize that debt was never the enemy. It was a teacher. It showed you how powerful your choices can be, for better or worse.

Smart debt teaches discipline. It reminds you to calculate before you commit. It helps you measure risk, not avoid it. It gives you structure. It builds resilience. Every time you borrow with purpose and repay with consistency, you prove to yourself that you can be trusted with responsibility.

There will always be people who tell you that all debt is bad. There will also be people who treat debt like free money. Both extremes miss the point. Debt is neutral until you give it direction. It is dangerous only when you let it lead.

The healthiest place to live is in balance. You understand how to use credit without being consumed by it. You can leverage debt when it multiplies your potential and avoid it when it only multiplies your stress. You learn to borrow from confidence, not from fear.

Freedom from dumb debt does not mean never borrowing again. It means that when you do, it is a decision, not a reaction. It means that you can look at what you owe and know exactly why it exists. It means that every loan, every card, every payment fits inside a plan that you control.

When you reach that point, something powerful happens. The guilt disappears. The anxiety quiets. The same numbers that once felt heavy begin to feel manageable. You start to see debt for what it really is, a temporary agreement between who you were and who you are becoming.

The moment you treat it that way, you stop being afraid of it. You start learning from it. You begin to use it with wisdom and purpose. You stop asking, "How fast can I get rid of it?" and start asking, "How can I make sure it never owns me again?"

That mindset is what separates financial peace from financial pressure. It is not the absence of debt that creates freedom. It is the presence of control. It is the awareness that no matter what you owe, you are still the one deciding what happens next.

Making money work for you means understanding every tool available, including debt. When used wisely, it can build bridges. When used carelessly, it builds walls. The choice is yours.

The path to freedom is not perfection. It is clarity. It is the daily choice to live with intention. To borrow when it builds and to walk away when it binds. To keep leading your money, even when it takes longer than you hoped.

In the end, debt is just another form of energy. You can spend it or you can invest it. You can waste it or you can work it. But one thing is certain. It will always follow your direction.

Make sure that direction leads you somewhere worth going.

FOURTEEN

Invest Like an Adult

At some point, you have to decide whether you want your money to sit quietly or start working. Saving is a good beginning, but saving alone will never create freedom. It keeps you safe, but it does not make you secure. Safety protects you from loss. Security prepares you for the future. The difference between the two is investing.

Investing can sound intimidating. The very word makes some people tense. They imagine complexity, risk, or luck. They picture people glued to screens, trying to predict what will happen next. But investing does not have to be mysterious. It is simply the process of letting your money participate in growth. It is how you move from working for money to letting money work for you.

The truth is that you are already investing in something. Every time you spend your time, energy, or attention, you are investing. You are planting seeds in the soil of your choices. The question is not whether you invest. It is whether you invest wisely.

When it comes to money, most people fall into one of two groups. The first is paralyzed by fear. They worry that they will make a mistake, so they do nothing. They tell themselves they will start when they learn more, when they have more, or when things calm down. But the right time never comes. Their caution feels wise, but it quietly costs them the most valuable resource of all: time.

The second group moves too fast. They chase trends, take advice from strangers online, and gamble on what feels exciting. They mistake motion for progress. Their confidence looks bold, but it is really impulsive. They win sometimes, but they lose more often. Both groups are driven by emotion instead of education.

To invest like an adult is to find the middle path. It means trading emotion for understanding. It means being patient instead of paralyzed, and disciplined instead of desperate. It means remembering that investing is not a game. It is stewardship.

When I first started investing, I thought it was about finding the perfect strategy. I studied charts, compared funds, and tried to outthink the market. I made progress, but I also made mistakes. What I learned through experience is that the most important skill in investing is not prediction. It is patience. You do not have to be a genius to build wealth. You only have to stay consistent long enough for compounding to do its work.

Investing like an adult is about building a relationship with time. It is about understanding that short-term excitement often sacrifices long-term growth. The more mature you become financially, the less you chase quick wins. You stop asking, "How fast can I double my money?" and start asking, "How can I make sure my money keeps growing for the next twenty years?"

The key to this mindset is purpose. Every investment you make should have a reason. You are not throwing darts at opportunity. You are building a structure that supports your goals. Maybe your purpose is security, or freedom, or legacy. Whatever it is, let it guide your decisions. When you know your why, the how becomes simpler.

Another mark of maturity is learning to accept volatility without panic. Markets rise and fall. They always have, and they always will. The immature investor reacts emotionally to every dip and surge. The mature investor stays calm. They understand that value does not vanish just because price fluctuates. They know that long-term growth always includes short-term noise.

There is a peace that comes from understanding this. You begin to see investing not as gambling, but as gardening. You plant seeds, you nurture them, and you wait. Some grow quickly, others slowly, but they all grow when you stay consistent. The soil of time does not reward impatience. It rewards faithfulness.

Investing also teaches humility. You cannot control the market, the economy, or the timing of opportunity. You can only control your behavior. You can decide to keep showing up. You can keep learning. You can stay consistent when others quit. That is how wealth is built quietly, not through luck, but through discipline.

Many people think investing begins with money. It doesn't. It begins with mindset. You can learn strategies later, but first you must develop the patience to handle delayed gratification. You must learn to see progress in decades, not days. You must accept that stability is more valuable than speed.

The truth is that every investment carries risk. But the greater risk is doing nothing. Inflation, missed opportunity, and fear will quietly erode your future if you let them. Investing is not about eliminating risk. It is about learning to manage it wisely. It is about putting your money into places where it can grow faster than time can shrink it.

You do not need to become an expert. You need to become consistent. The average person who invests faithfully in simple, low-cost funds over time will outperform the majority of people who chase complicated strategies. Simplicity wins because it allows consistency.

Investing like an adult is also about emotional control. You will be tempted to compare your

progress to others. You will see stories of
people who seem to be getting rich overnight.
You will question whether you are doing
enough. Those moments are tests of maturity.
You do not need to chase their path. You only
need to stay on yours.

Over time, your focus shifts from excitement to
endurance. You stop measuring success by
speed and start measuring it by peace. You
understand that investing is not just about
building wealth. It is about building character.
It develops patience, perspective, and wisdom.

When you reach this level of understanding, you
begin to see how everything connects. Your
income, your savings, your investments, your
habits—they are all part of one system. When
you treat each part with care, they begin to
work together. You are no longer reacting to
money. You are directing it.

That is what it means to invest like an adult. It
is not about playing it safe or taking big risks. It
is about learning to think long-term. It is about
being steady in uncertainty and confident in
simplicity. It is about taking responsibility for
your future instead of hoping someone else will
handle it for you.

Investing is not a race. It is a relationship with time. The longer you stay faithful, the stronger it becomes.

When you finally understand that, investing stops feeling like pressure. It starts feeling like partnership. You begin to trust the process. You stop worrying about every fluctuation and start focusing on what you can control. You build peace through patience.

That is what it means to invest with maturity. You do not chase what shines. You build what lasts.

And over time, you discover that investing was never just about money. It was about becoming the kind of person who can handle abundance without losing balance.

FIFTEEN

Insurance, Wills, and What No One Talks About

Most people spend their entire lives building something and never stop to protect it. They work hard, save faithfully, and plan for the future, yet they leave the most fragile parts of that future uncovered. It is not because they do not care. It is because these conversations make them uncomfortable.

No one enjoys thinking about loss, injury, or death. These are the subjects that live in the quiet corners of life, the ones we tell ourselves we will get to later. But later has a way of coming faster than we expect. The truth is, real financial maturity is not only about growing what you have. It is about protecting it.

Insurance and estate planning are not exciting. They are not glamorous or motivational. But they are essential. They are how you turn effort into endurance. They are what make sure that the work you are doing today still matters tomorrow.

I avoided these topics for a long time. I told myself I was too young, too healthy, too busy. The idea of sitting down to talk about life insurance or a will felt unnecessary, almost superstitious. I thought that planning for the worst might somehow invite it. What I learned later is that avoiding these conversations does not prevent difficulty. It just leaves you unprepared for it.

Peace does not come from pretending bad things will never happen. It comes from knowing you can handle them if they do.

Insurance exists for that reason. It is not a symbol of fear. It is a symbol of foresight. It is the quiet agreement that says, "I have thought ahead. I care about the people who depend on me. I refuse to let my absence create chaos."

The purpose of insurance is simple. It transfers risk. It protects your family from losing what they could not replace. It ensures that your stability continues even when life does not go according to plan. You may never need it, but if you do, it will be the most important decision you ever made.

There are different kinds of protection, but they all serve the same purpose. Health insurance shields you from medical costs that can destroy your savings overnight. Life insurance replaces income so your family can breathe through grief instead of scrambling through it. Disability coverage provides support when your body cannot keep up with your ambition. These are not luxuries. They are layers of love disguised as paperwork.

Having protection does not mean you are pessimistic. It means you are responsible. It means you are mature enough to face what could go wrong without letting fear control what you do next.

The same principle applies to wills and estate planning. Many people assume these things are only for the wealthy. They imagine lawyers, assets, and complicated documents. In reality, every person needs a plan, no matter their income. A will is not about wealth. It is about clarity. It is about making sure that your values are carried out when you are no longer here to explain them.

A will is an act of kindness. It removes confusion for the people you love most. It gives direction when emotions are high and logic is clouded. It spares your family from unnecessary decisions during an already difficult time. It is your voice preserved in writing, ensuring that what you built and what you care about are handled with care.

If you have ever lost someone close to you, you know how heavy those first few weeks can feel. The emotional weight is already unbearable. Adding financial confusion on top of it makes everything harder. That is what planning prevents. It gives your loved ones space to grieve instead of scramble.

For many people, the hesitation to plan comes from discomfort. Talking about death feels final. It forces us to confront what we would rather not think about. But pretending something will not happen has never stopped it from happening. It only removes our ability to influence the outcome.

When you take time to prepare, you give your future self and your family a gift. You create security that outlives you. You make sure that your money, your home, your work, and your values stay aligned even when you are gone. That is what legacy really is. It is not about how much you leave. It is about how well you leave it.

There is another reason people avoid this step. It feels complicated. They do not know where to start. But most of the time, it is simpler than they think. You can begin by writing down what you own, what you owe, and who depends on you. You can decide who should handle your affairs and what you want to happen with the things you have built. Then you put it in writing and make it official. That small act turns confusion into clarity.

The deeper truth here is that planning for the future is not just about money. It is about peace. It is about the quiet strength that comes from knowing that you have done what you can. It is about reducing the emotional burden on the people who love you. It is a way of saying, "I cared enough to make this easier for you."

When I finally sat down to organize my own plan, something shifted inside me. What began as a task I had been avoiding turned into one of the most freeing experiences of my life. For the first time, I could see the whole picture of what I had built. I realized how far I had come and how much of my effort could now live beyond me. It gave me a sense of closure, not in the morbid sense, but in the peaceful one.

Planning for the unexpected does not make life smaller. It makes it stronger. It allows you to live more fully because you know you have already taken care of the what-ifs. You can focus on the present without worrying about the future. You can give without fear because you have already protected what matters most.

That is the real purpose of this kind of planning. It is not paperwork. It is peace of mind. It is stewardship extended into the future. It ensures that your family is not left with confusion or chaos. It keeps your story intact even after you stop writing it.

Most people will never talk openly about insurance, wills, or planning. These are not the topics that make headlines or inspire excitement. But they are the topics that make life work. They are what keep love intact when life changes suddenly.

There is a quiet confidence that comes from having everything in order. You sleep better. You breathe easier. You walk through life knowing that the people you care about will be cared for. That is not fear. That is faith in action.

Showing up financially is not just about earning, saving, or investing. It is about protecting what you build. It is about thinking ahead not because you expect the worst, but because you are wise enough to plan for it.

When you finally have these pieces in place, you will understand what peace truly feels like. It is not the absence of risk. It is the presence of preparation. It is the knowledge that you have done what you can, and that is enough.

That is what no one talks about. But it is what everyone deserves to feel.

SIXTEEN

The Freedom Formula

Freedom is a word people love to use, but few ever stop to define it. It is one of those ideas that sounds simple until you try to live it. Everyone wants to feel free, yet most spend their lives confined by invisible walls. Some are trapped by debt, others by fear, and many by the belief that more will finally make them safe.

But freedom is not a number. It is not something you reach when your account balance hits a certain mark. It is not waiting on a promotion, a business win, or the next big financial milestone. Freedom begins the moment you stop being controlled by money and start directing it with purpose.

That is the real formula. Freedom equals clarity plus control. It is knowing what you need, managing it well, and refusing to be ruled by what you earn. It is the quiet confidence that comes from being able to make choices without panic.

Most people chase freedom through addition. They think they need to earn more, buy more, build more. But freedom is often subtraction. It is removing what weighs you down. It is cutting out unnecessary obligations, draining expenses, and false expectations. It is saying no to the noise so you can say yes to what matters.

When you begin to understand this, everything about your financial life starts to change. You no longer chase status. You chase peace. You stop comparing your situation to others because you realize that their version of freedom might look nothing like yours.

The Freedom Formula is not about escaping work. It is about transforming your relationship with it. Work becomes a choice, not a sentence. It becomes something you do with intention instead of obligation. You still work hard, but it feels different. You are building, not begging. You are leading, not surviving.

I learned this through experience. For years, I equated success with movement. I believed that slowing down meant falling behind. I filled every hour, convinced that productivity was proof of progress. What I eventually realized was that I was not chasing purpose. I was running from fear. I was afraid that if I stopped pushing, everything would collapse.

When I finally began to slow down, I discovered that my life did not fall apart. It opened up. I had more time, more clarity, and more presence. My work improved because I was no longer working from exhaustion. That was the beginning of real freedom.

Money can buy a lot of things, but it cannot buy that feeling. You can purchase comfort, but not contentment. You can buy space, but not peace. The only way to experience both is to learn the discipline of enough. To know when to stop striving and start living.

That is what the Freedom Formula protects. It is not about the constant pursuit of more. It is about creating stability that allows you to rest. It is about using money to support your life, not define it.

To live free, you must first know what you are serving. If your decisions are still shaped by fear, you will always feel limited. You can have a large income and still feel poor if you believe that security comes from control. But when you let go of that need to grip so tightly, you create space for peace to enter.

Freedom also requires responsibility. It is not a careless lifestyle. It is intentional. It means you plan your finances so that your choices reflect your values. It means you give as easily as you save, because you understand that money is meant to move through you, not just to you. It means you are honest about what matters and willing to let go of what doesn't.

The formula for freedom is simple, but it demands awareness. First, you define what freedom means for you. Not in theory, but in detail. What does a peaceful life look like? How much does it cost? How much time do you want to protect? Who do you want to serve? Once you have clarity, you align your resources to that vision.

Then comes control. Not control in the sense of perfection, but in the sense of leadership. You decide how your money behaves. You manage it with purpose instead of panic. You stop letting it react to the world around you and start giving it clear direction.

This combination creates confidence. You stop chasing financial peace and start creating it. You stop waiting for circumstances to calm down and start calming them yourself. The freedom you once thought required wealth now comes from wisdom.

The truth is that most people overcomplicate money. They try to master systems before mastering themselves. But you cannot have financial freedom without emotional freedom. The two are connected. The more peace you have inside, the less chaos you create outside.

Once you learn this, you stop viewing money as the destination. You start seeing it as a means to something greater. It becomes a resource for time, generosity, and presence. It becomes a way to build a life that feels good on the inside, not just one that looks good from the outside.

I have seen people with very little live in complete peace because they understand this truth. I have also seen people with abundance live in constant tension because they do not. The difference is not in the numbers. It is in the mindset.

Freedom is a decision long before it is a condition. It begins the day you decide that your peace is worth more than your possessions. It begins when you stop proving your worth through your work and start protecting your time with wisdom.

The Freedom Formula is not complicated. It is built on small, steady habits that stack together. You earn, you save, you give, you protect, and you rest. You live with clarity and consistency. You create systems that serve you. And in doing so, you build a life that cannot be shaken by financial storms.

The moment you stop chasing freedom and start practicing it, you realize it was never as far away as it seemed. It was waiting for you to stop running and start leading.

When you understand this formula, your entire view of success changes. You no longer measure it in dollars or possessions. You measure it in mornings that feel calm, evenings that feel peaceful, and relationships that feel whole. You begin to see that the real reward of showing up financially is not wealth. It is wisdom.

Freedom is not something you earn. It is something you learn.

And once you do, you carry it with you everywhere you go.

SEVENTEEN

The Bigger Picture of Wealth

At some point, you realize that money alone cannot measure your success. It can provide comfort, opportunity, and convenience, but it cannot fill the spaces that truly matter. It cannot repair a relationship, restore peace of mind, or create purpose. Those things come from the way you live, not the way you earn.

Most people spend years chasing financial goals without stopping to ask what they are really building. They say they want wealth, but what they really want is what they think wealth will give them. They want security, respect, rest, or the ability to say yes without guilt. But money by itself does not create those things. It simply amplifies what already exists.

If your life feels chaotic before you have money, more money will only increase that chaos. If your life feels aligned, more money will increase that alignment. The difference is not in your income. It is in your integrity.

Real wealth is not measured in numbers. It is measured in harmony. It is what happens when your financial world supports every other part of your life instead of stealing from it.

The goal of all this work—the saving, the investing, the budgeting, the planning—is not just to get rich. It is to become whole.

Money touches everything, but it should never control everything. It should serve your relationships, your health, your purpose, and your peace. When you manage it with intention, it begins to strengthen those areas instead of competing with them. When you neglect it, it quietly erodes them.

I learned this truth the hard way. There was a season when I had reached many of my financial goals but felt less fulfilled than ever. I was proud of what I had built, but I was tired. I had achieved the kind of stability I once dreamed of, yet my relationships were thin, my body was exhausted, and my spirit felt disconnected. That was when I began to understand that wealth without wellness is just a more comfortable form of emptiness.

That realization changed everything. I began to see money differently. It stopped being the destination and started becoming a tool for balance. I started asking myself a simple question: "Is this decision creating peace or stealing it?" That single question became the filter for how I used my time, energy, and resources.

True financial health is about integration. It is not something you build apart from your life. It is something you build into your life. It should give you more time with your family, not take it away. It should help you contribute to something bigger than yourself, not isolate you. It should free your mind to focus on what matters, not fill it with endless worry.

When you begin to view wealth this way, you stop separating money from meaning. You stop asking, "How much do I have?" and start asking, "How well am I living?" You begin to measure abundance not by accumulation but by alignment.

That is what it means to show up more financially. It is not about being perfect with money. It is about being present with it. It is about understanding that every financial decision has emotional, relational, and spiritual weight.

When you spend, you are expressing what you value. When you save, you are expressing what you hope for. When you give, you are expressing what you believe in. Every transaction tells a story about who you are becoming.

Money itself is neutral, but your choices are not. They reveal what you prioritize. They show where your trust lies. When those choices are aligned with your deeper values, money becomes an ally. When they are not, it becomes a distraction.

The bigger picture of wealth is not just about financial independence. It is about personal integrity. It is about knowing that you are the same person in every area of your life. You do not pursue success at the expense of your health. You do not build abundance by sacrificing connection. You do not accumulate more while losing yourself in the process.

There is a kind of wealth that looks small on paper but feels rich in practice. It is the wealth of waking up with gratitude instead of stress. It is the wealth of being able to give freely because you have managed wisely. It is the wealth of knowing that your success has not come at the cost of your soul.

That kind of wealth is rare because it requires reflection. It asks you to slow down and examine what your money is actually doing for you. It asks you to redefine success in a world that constantly tells you it is never enough.

When you start to think this way, money becomes lighter. It stops carrying the weight of your identity. You begin to experience it as something fluid, something that moves through your life with purpose. It comes and goes, but your peace remains steady.

This is the stage of maturity where you stop trying to master money and start partnering with it. You see that the real goal is not to control it completely but to align it with your calling. Money becomes a reflection of your stewardship, your wisdom, and your heart.

That is what real prosperity looks like. It is not measured by how much you have, but by how many areas of your life are thriving at the same time. It is not limited to your bank account. It extends to your relationships, your health, your creativity, and your faith.

When all of those things work together, money finally takes its rightful place. It is no longer a source of stress or pride. It is simply a part of the rhythm of your life. You earn it, manage it, and release it with purpose. You live from peace instead of pressure.

Wealth is not about escaping responsibility. It is about expanding it. It is about using what you have been given to make life better—not just for yourself, but for others. It is about remembering that everything you build is borrowed time and borrowed opportunity. You are here to multiply it, not hoard it.

When you reach that point, you begin to experience a kind of abundance that no number can quantify. You feel content, capable, and connected. You know that your money, your work, and your values are finally speaking the same language.

That is the bigger picture of wealth. It is not about having everything. It is about being whole.

And that is the truest kind of financial freedom there is.

EIGHTEEN

Living Open-Handed

Money is meant to move. It flows in and out like a tide, sometimes calm, sometimes strong, but always moving. When you try to grip it too tightly, it slips through your fingers. When you learn to hold it open-handed, it begins to serve you instead of scare you.

Generosity is one of the clearest signs of financial maturity. It is the point where fear and control give way to trust and purpose. You stop asking, "What can I keep?" and start asking, "What can I contribute?" That shift changes everything. It turns money from a symbol of anxiety into a tool of peace.

Living open-handed does not mean giving irresponsibly. It means understanding that money multiplies meaning when it moves. It means recognizing that generosity is not just about dollars. It is about posture. It is about the way you see the world and your place in it.

For most of us, learning to give begins with discomfort. We hesitate because we have lived through seasons of scarcity. We know what it feels like to not have enough, so we hold on tightly even when we could let go. We tell ourselves that we will give when things are more stable, when the timing is better, when we have more. But that moment rarely comes.

The truth is that generosity is not a by-product of wealth. It is a choice of perspective. It starts small. It starts when you decide that you already have something to offer. It grows when you realize that giving does not create lack. It creates life.

When I first started giving consistently, I did it out of obligation. I thought it was something I was supposed to do, a rule to follow. But over time, it changed me. I noticed how it loosened my fear. Each time I gave, I felt lighter. I realized that generosity was not about what left my hand. It was about what left my heart. The tension, the worry, the constant sense of scarcity began to fade. I discovered that giving was not losing. It was releasing.

Living open-handed requires trust. You have to believe that the same force that brought resources into your life once can do it again. You have to believe that you will not run out. That belief is not blind optimism. It is recognition. You have already made it through seasons where you thought you wouldn't. You have already survived moments when you had less. If you can trust yourself to rebuild once, you can trust yourself again.

Generosity strengthens that trust. It builds faith in the cycle of giving and receiving. It teaches you that money, like water, stagnates when it stops moving. The more you circulate it with purpose, the healthier it becomes. The more you cling to it, the heavier it feels.

There is a peace that comes from knowing that your security does not live in your savings account. Savings matter, but they are not the source of safety. Peace comes from clarity, from consistency, from the ability to know that you are acting with integrity. When you live open-handed, your confidence shifts from the balance of your account to the balance of your actions.

Generosity also breaks pride. It reminds you that money is not a scoreboard. It humbles you in the best way. It reconnects you to people, to purpose, and to gratitude. It makes you aware of how fortunate you already are. That awareness produces perspective. And perspective is what keeps you free.

Giving should not feel like guilt. It should feel like gratitude. It is not about how much you give, but how much peace it brings. When you give with fear, it feels like loss. When you give with love, it feels like alignment.

I once met a man who had very little but gave often. He told me that he could not imagine living any other way. When I asked him how he managed to give so freely, he said, "Because I never lost anything I was meant to keep." That sentence has stayed with me. It reframed everything I thought I understood about generosity.

Living open-handed does not mean ignoring wisdom. You still plan, save, and prepare. But your planning is rooted in trust, not control. You know that money will come and go, but your values remain steady. You do not give because you can afford to. You give because you are free to.

When you live this way, money starts to lose its grip on your emotions. You stop seeing it as something to hoard and start seeing it as something to steward. You realize that the more freely you move it, the more peace you keep. The more you share, the more capable you feel.

Generosity is not just an act of kindness. It is an act of strength. It reminds you that you have enough, that you are enough, and that you are part of something bigger than your own balance sheet.

When you give, you build invisible bridges. You connect your work to the wellbeing of others. You turn effort into impact. And in that process, your financial life gains meaning beyond measurement.

The habit of giving also protects you from fear. When the world feels uncertain, generosity anchors you. It reminds you that abundance is not something you wait for. It is something you create. You begin to trust that as long as you continue to move money with integrity, you will always have what you need.

Over time, generosity becomes second nature. It stops feeling like a separate part of your

financial plan and becomes part of your
identity. You do not give to fix your conscience.
You give because it feels natural to contribute.
You give because it feels right to be part of the
flow of something greater than yourself.

When you live open-handed, your definition of
wealth expands. It is no longer limited to what
you keep. It includes what you give. It includes
the peace that comes from knowing that your
money is making life better, even in small ways.

That is the deeper purpose of financial growth.
Not to build bigger walls, but to open wider
doors. Not to insulate yourself from others, but
to include them in your blessings.

You will find that when you give freely, life gives
back in unexpected ways. Not always in money,
but in peace, perspective, and connection.
Those are the returns that matter most.

Living open-handed is the final stage of
financial freedom. It is the point where money
no longer owns you at all. It flows through your
life with purpose and grace. You no longer
measure success by what you have gained, but
by what you have given.

Because the real reward of financial health is not wealth. It is the freedom to be generous without fear.

And that freedom will always come back to you multiplied in peace.

NINETEEN

Rich vs. Wealthy

At first glance, the words "rich" and "wealthy" sound the same. People use them interchangeably, as if they describe the same destination reached by different routes. But they are not the same. They describe two entirely different ways of living, thinking, and relating to money.

To be rich is to have a lot. To be wealthy is to need less.

Rich is a status. Wealthy is a state of being.

You can be rich for a season, but you can only be wealthy by design.

Rich people chase money. Wealthy people attract peace.

The difference is not in the amount of money, but in the amount of freedom that money creates. Rich is loud. Wealthy is quiet. Rich buys what it can. Wealthy protects what matters.

Most people never stop to think about the difference because the world celebrates rich. It sells the image of luxury and labels it success. But rich can be fragile. It often depends on constant motion—income, attention, validation. Wealth, on the other hand, depends on intention. It endures even when life slows down.

Rich lives for the next big thing. Wealthy learns to enjoy what already is.

Being rich is about appearance. Being wealthy is about alignment.

When I was younger, I used to equate the two. I thought if I could just make enough, I would automatically feel secure. But no matter how much I earned, I kept feeling the same restlessness. The pressure never left. The bills grew, the lifestyle grew, and the expectations grew with them. I was chasing peace through progress, but I could never catch it.

That is the hidden cost of being rich. You can have everything and still feel empty because you are measuring success with the wrong ruler.

Wealthy people think differently. They build lives that feel full, not just look full. They value time as much as income. They invest in relationships, health, and peace with the same discipline they bring to their finances. They measure success by how free they feel, not how impressed others are.

To be rich is to ask, "How much can I get?" To be wealthy is to ask, "How much can I sustain?"

Rich can be lost overnight. Wealthy is built slowly and intentionally.

Rich depends on income. Wealthy depends on wisdom.

You can tell the difference by how a person reacts when money changes. The rich panic when the flow slows down because their identity depends on it. The wealthy adjust, because they have built their life on purpose, not performance.

I once met someone who made an incredible amount of money but could not sleep. Every decision felt high-stakes. Every expense carried guilt. They had resources most people dream of, yet lived in constant fear of losing it all. I also met another person who earned modestly but lived freely. Their bills were paid, their days were simple, and their heart was light. The first was rich. The second was wealthy.

The more you grow financially, the more important this distinction becomes. If you do not understand it, you risk building a life that owns you. Rich can happen by accident. Wealthy never does. It requires intention. It requires restraint. It requires the courage to say no when the world keeps saying more.

The rich use money to prove something. The wealthy use money to protect something.

For the rich, money is a mirror. It reflects identity. For the wealthy, money is a tool. It reflects stewardship.

You can see this difference in how people spend. Rich people often buy to be seen. Wealthy people buy for sustainability. Rich focuses on image. Wealthy focuses on impact.

The goal is not to shame success or luxury. There is nothing wrong with nice things. The problem begins when the things start owning the person. When the image of success becomes more important than the reality of peace. When the external wins come at the expense of the internal ones.

That is why wealthy people understand the value of "enough." They know that peace begins where pressure ends. They build margin into their lives, not just in their budgets. They design systems that serve them instead of enslave them. They build stability quietly, in ways that do not require constant attention.

The rich are often fueled by competition. The wealthy are fueled by contribution.

The rich chase recognition. The wealthy chase legacy.

The difference is subtle, but it changes everything.

Being rich is about accumulation. Being wealthy is about appreciation.

The moment you shift from one to the other, your relationship with money changes completely. You stop counting what you have and start noticing what you value. You begin to understand that the goal is not to build a bigger life. It is to build a better one.

Wealth is not about having more money. It is about having more choices. More time. More peace. More presence. It is about waking up and knowing that your day belongs to you.

That kind of freedom cannot be bought. It has to be built—through stewardship, awareness, and discipline. It grows in the small daily decisions that reflect your priorities. It shows up in the quiet moments when you choose peace over pressure.

When you understand this difference, you stop striving for rich and start cultivating wealth. You stop letting ego make your decisions. You stop needing to prove your value. You begin to trust that peace is proof enough.

That is the turning point for most people. It is the moment they realize that wealth has less to do with numbers and more to do with alignment. You can earn ten times more and still feel poor if your life is out of balance. You can earn far less and feel abundant if your values, habits, and heart are in sync.

Wealthy is not what you see. It is what you feel when the noise goes quiet.

When you live this way, you no longer have to chase money. You attract it by living in integrity. You spend it wisely because you are not trying to fill a void. You use it purposefully because you know what matters.

That is the final stage of maturity with money. You are no longer controlled by it. You are in partnership with it. It serves your purpose instead of competing with it.

The world will always push you toward rich. It will tell you that you are falling behind, that success means more, that happiness lives in what is next. But you will know better. You will know that true wealth is not about having everything. It is about having peace no matter what you have.

Rich ends with more. Wealthy ends with enough.

And enough will always be where freedom begins.

TWENTY

Redefining Wealth

At some point, every person has to decide what wealth really means to them. Not what the world says it should mean, not what your parents believed it meant, but what it means for you. Because if you never define it, someone else will.

The world is loud about money. It shouts numbers and titles. It tells you to measure your worth by what you own, where you live, and how much you earn. It sells the idea that wealth equals happiness, and that success is found in the next milestone. But the longer you chase that version of wealth, the more you realize it is an illusion. It always stays just out of reach.

Real wealth is quiet. It does not need to be displayed to be felt. It lives in the peace of knowing you have enough, in the strength of being content, and in the joy of living aligned with your values.

The journey through this book has been about that kind of wealth. It began with awareness—seeing the ways money controlled your emotions and decisions. Then it became about stewardship, discipline, and growth. But beneath it all, the goal has never been to get rich. The goal has been to become well.

Because wealth without wellness is not wealth at all. It is imbalance dressed up as achievement. You can have every luxury in the world and still feel poor if your heart is anxious, your relationships are thin, and your peace depends on performance.

Redefining wealth means rewriting what you believe success looks like. It means stepping off the treadmill of comparison and deciding that your version of abundance can look simple. It can look quiet. It can look like stability instead of extravagance. It can look like time instead of things.

When you begin to see wealth this way, you stop chasing it and start cultivating it. You realize that true prosperity is built from the inside out. It begins with gratitude. It grows through generosity. It sustains itself through balance.

Wealth, at its core, is not about accumulation. It is about capacity. It is about how much peace, joy, and meaning your life can hold. It is about being rich in presence, not just possessions.

I remember a time when I was earning more than I ever thought I would, yet I felt empty. I was always busy, always planning, always chasing the next thing. The numbers looked good, but my soul felt poor. It took time to understand that I had built a successful life by every external standard but had failed to build one that felt whole.

That realization forced me to slow down and look at what wealth actually was for me. It was not the size of my account or the price of my house. It was my ability to be present with my family. It was having time to think, space to rest, and freedom to give. It was waking up without a knot of anxiety in my chest. It was feeling proud, not pressured.

When you define wealth that way, your entire relationship with money changes. It stops being the goal and becomes the vehicle. You use it to build peace instead of identity. You use it to support what matters most. You begin to make decisions not based on status but on sustainability.

That is what maturity looks like in finance. It is not mastering the stock market. It is mastering yourself. It is knowing when to say enough, when to slow down, and when to enjoy what you have already built. It is understanding that success is not about being ahead of others. It is about being aligned with yourself.

The most powerful people I have ever met are not the ones with the most money. They are the ones with the most peace. They walk lightly. They do not need to prove anything. They know what matters to them and what does not. They are not pulled by every new trend or shaken by every small loss. Their wealth is not in what they control, but in what they have learned to release.

That kind of wealth cannot be taken away. It does not depend on markets, jobs, or circumstances. It lives inside you. It is built through clarity, patience, and purpose. It is built by showing up consistently for your values, your people, and your life.

When you redefine wealth this way, you start seeing opportunities everywhere. A conversation with your child becomes wealth. A quiet morning without worry becomes wealth. The ability to give freely becomes wealth. The peace of knowing your bills are covered and your time is your own becomes wealth.

You realize that you have probably been wealthier than you thought all along. You were just measuring it with the wrong metrics.

This perspective shift also brings relief. You stop trying to compete in a race that never ends. You start living at a pace that actually fits you. You find joy in stewardship instead of striving. You appreciate the simple things again. You learn that success can be gentle.

Redefining wealth does not mean rejecting ambition. It means aligning it. You can still want more, but your reasons change. You are no longer chasing more to fill a void. You are pursuing more because you have something meaningful to grow. Your work, your income, your goals—all of it begins to feel lighter because you are building from peace, not pressure.

When you live from this place, wealth becomes an act of contribution. You use it to help others, to create opportunities, to make a difference. It becomes a reflection of gratitude instead of greed. You stop asking, "What can I get?" and start asking, "What can I give?"

The irony is that when you reach this mindset, money begins to work more easily. Decisions are simpler. Spending feels intentional. Earning feels fulfilling. You make better choices because you are no longer driven by fear. That is the secret no one talks about. When you stop letting money define you, it finally starts working for you.

Redefining wealth is not a one-time event. It is a continual process of alignment. Life will change. Your priorities will shift. What feels like abundance today may look different in ten years. The goal is not to find a permanent definition but to keep checking in with yourself

and asking if your money still reflects your
values.

True wealth is a living thing. It grows as you do.
It matures as you learn. It expands as your heart
opens. And when you look back, you will see
that the richest seasons of your life were not the
ones when you earned the most, but the ones
when you lived the most.

Wealth is not what you have. It is how you live.

And once you understand that, you will never
measure it the same way again.

TWENTY-ONE

Building Systems That Serve You

Wisdom without structure eventually fades. You can have all the clarity and conviction in the world, but if your daily systems do not support your values, life will pull you back to old patterns.

That is why the most successful people are not always the most talented. They are the most consistent. They have built systems that make it easier to do what matters and harder to drift away from it. Systems protect peace. They keep your life aligned when energy runs low.

A financial system is not just a budget. It is a rhythm. It is how you make sure that your money follows your values automatically. It is how you protect your progress from chaos.

For years, I thought structure meant restriction. I resisted systems because I wanted to stay flexible. I told myself that freedom meant having options, not routines. But the truth is, lack of structure is not freedom. It is fatigue. It forces you to make the same decisions over and over again. You wake up each day starting from zero.

When I finally built clear systems, I realized how much energy I had been wasting. Automation replaced anxiety. Planning replaced panic. I no longer had to think about every little detail because the structure carried it for me. That is when I understood that systems do not limit you. They support you.

A good system turns discipline into default. It allows your values to operate even when your motivation disappears. It makes consistency easier than inconsistency. It creates calm by replacing decision fatigue with direction.

Building a financial system that serves you begins with intention. You decide what matters most and build around it. You set up automation for saving, giving, and investing. You create boundaries for spending. You simplify accounts so you can see your situation clearly. You make sure every part of your financial life has a purpose and a place.

These systems do not have to be complicated. They just have to be consistent. The goal is not to design a machine. It is to create a rhythm that keeps you in alignment. It should feel natural, not forced.

Once you set it up, your financial life becomes lighter. You stop reacting. You start leading. Your system does the heavy lifting so you can focus on what matters most. You still check in, you still make adjustments, but you are no longer fighting fires every week. You are steering the ship instead of patching leaks.

The beauty of systems is that they protect you from both chaos and emotion. When you have a clear plan, you do not have to rely on willpower. You can let your systems act on your behalf. The savings transfer happens. The investment continues. The giving goes out. Your progress no longer depends on how you feel that day.

Systems also create accountability. They remind you of who you are and who you are becoming. Each automated decision is a reflection of your priorities. It says, "This is what I stand for. This is what I'm building."

When your systems reflect your values, money becomes peaceful again. You are not constantly adjusting, fixing, or apologizing. You are maintaining order. You are practicing stewardship. You are living with awareness instead of avoidance.

This kind of structure does not remove spontaneity. It makes it possible. When you know your essentials are handled, you can enjoy the unexpected without guilt. You can take a trip, give generously, or rest deeply because your base is secure. That is real freedom.

Without systems, freedom feels fragile. With them, freedom becomes sustainable.

I often tell people that if you want to feel financially strong, do not chase perfection. Build systems that can handle your humanity. Expect that there will be weeks when you are tired, distracted, or unmotivated. Your systems are what carry you through those moments.

They keep your goals alive while you catch your breath.

The best systems are simple enough to maintain but strong enough to protect. They should fit your lifestyle, not fight it. They should make good decisions easier and bad ones less convenient. They should serve your life, not control it.

You can always refine them as you grow. What matters most is that you begin. Once your systems are in motion, they start building momentum on their own. They create habits. Those habits create results. And results create confidence.

That confidence extends beyond money. When you know you have order in one area, it strengthens every other area. You carry that peace into your relationships, your work, and your health. You realize that systems are not just for finance. They are a way of showing up for life.

When you live this way, you stop trying to manage everything manually. You start trusting the processes you have built. You check in regularly, but you do not hover. You understand that leadership is not control. It is design.

Eventually, you begin to notice something beautiful. Your life starts to feel predictable in the best way. You are no longer ruled by fear or reaction. You can breathe. You can plan. You can rest. Your systems quietly hold you in place so you can focus on purpose instead of pressure.

That is when you know they are working.

Building systems that serve you is not about creating perfection. It is about creating peace. It is about designing a framework that allows your best intentions to become your normal behavior. It is about protecting your progress so you can keep growing even when life gets hard.

The goal is not to build systems for the sake of order. It is to build systems that give you more life. Systems that create margin for meaning. Systems that make space for joy.

Once you experience that, you will never go back to winging it. You will understand that freedom without structure is chaos, and structure without freedom is prison. True peace lives in the balance between them.

When your systems reflect that balance, you are no longer surviving your financial life. You are directing it. You are no longer reacting to circumstances. You are shaping them.

And in that rhythm, wealth stops being a destination. It becomes a way of living.

Because real success is not built in moments of motivation. It is built in the systems that carry you when motivation fades.

That is how you build a life that keeps working even when you are resting.

That is how you build systems that truly serve you.

TWENTY-TWO

When More Isn't Better

There is a quiet lie that most people live by. It sounds harmless, even inspiring. It says that more is always better. More money, more opportunity, more growth, more everything. It is a belief so woven into our culture that it feels like truth. But it is not.

More can be good, but more is not always better. In fact, sometimes more is the very thing that steals peace, blinds purpose, and destroys balance.

If you think about it, the pursuit of "more" has no finish line. You can always earn a little more, save a little more, buy a little more, accomplish a little more. And in that chase, you rarely stop to ask, "Better for what? Better for whom?"

The problem with "more" is that it never answers its own question. It just demands another round. It tells you that fulfillment is one achievement away. But once you reach that milestone, the satisfaction fades, and the chase begins again.

This is how people who appear successful on the outside can still feel empty. They have mastered accumulation but not alignment. They have everything they thought they wanted, yet somehow it still does not feel like enough.

I lived that pattern for years. Every time I hit a goal, I would raise it. Every win became a new baseline. I told myself it was ambition, but it was addiction. I could not sit still in contentment. I had confused growth with peace.

Eventually, the weight of "more" caught up to me. I realized that I had built a life that looked full but felt hollow. My schedule was packed, my income was high, but my energy was gone. I was succeeding in every visible way while failing in every invisible one. That was when I learned that the most dangerous part of success is forgetting to define enough.

Enough is not a lack of ambition. It is the boundary that protects your peace. It is the line between expansion and exhaustion. It is the difference between a full life and a frantic one.

When you define enough, you begin to see that growth is not just about addition. It is also about refinement. It is about removing what no longer serves you. It is about simplifying so that what remains can thrive.

True growth often looks like pruning. You cut back what is overgrown so the roots can strengthen. The same is true in your financial life. Sometimes you have to say no to new opportunities, even profitable ones, because they cost too much in energy or peace. Sometimes you have to let go of what looks good so you can protect what is actually good.

When you stop worshiping "more," you start appreciating "better." Better conversations. Better boundaries. Better health. Better rest. You start valuing depth over expansion. You begin to understand that quality of life is a richer metric than quantity of possessions.

The irony is that this shift does not make you lazy. It makes you sharper. You stop wasting effort on things that do not matter. You become more strategic, more present, and more alive. You focus your time and resources on what actually brings meaning instead of what just brings motion.

I used to think that slowing down meant falling behind. Now I see that slowing down is what allows you to get ahead in the ways that count. You cannot think clearly, lead well, or love deeply when you are sprinting through your life. Rest is not a reward for success. It is the foundation that makes success sustainable.

When you live with that awareness, you stop confusing busyness with progress. You start designing your financial life around what supports you, not what impresses others. You spend less energy chasing growth for its own sake and more energy protecting what matters. You stop building higher and start building deeper.

There is a peace that comes when you reach this point. You no longer feel pressured to prove yourself through productivity. You no longer measure your worth by your work. You begin to enjoy what you have built. You start to see that the purpose of financial wisdom is not constant expansion. It is stability. It is the ability to rest without fear and grow without greed.

This kind of maturity takes time. It goes against the messages you have been taught since childhood. You will be told that you are wasting potential, that you could do more, that you should always be hungry. But hunger without discernment leads to burnout. Ambition without rest becomes emptiness.

Learning when to stop is as important as learning how to start.

That is the secret of long-term peace. The discipline of restraint. The wisdom to know when you have reached enough and the courage to stay there.

You might think that holding back limits your potential. But the opposite is true. Restraint multiplies strength. When you focus on what matters most, you pour your energy into fewer things that produce greater returns. You stop scattering your life across too many pursuits and start mastering the ones that truly align with your purpose.

Financially, that might mean choosing a slower, steadier path instead of the one that promises faster growth. It might mean keeping your expenses stable even when your income rises. It might mean saying no to investments or opportunities that do not align with your values.

Whatever it looks like, the principle is the same. The goal is not to do everything. It is to do the right things well.

When you start living that way, you feel lighter. You notice how much peace was buried under all that striving. You realize that "more" was never the goal. Peace was. Presence was. Freedom was.

You start to see that the richest people are not the ones with the most money, but the ones with the fewest regrets. They know when to walk away. They know how to enjoy what they already have. They know that their worth does not depend on their next win.

The wisdom of "enough" does not kill ambition. It refines it. It gives ambition boundaries so it does not consume you. It teaches you to grow within your values instead of beyond them.

When you reach this point, your life begins to feel different. You wake up with a quieter mind. You make decisions without panic. You no longer feel like everything depends on the next breakthrough. You start to trust what you have built.

That is what financial peace really is. It is not a destination. It is a rhythm. It is knowing when to move and when to rest. It is trusting that you are already equipped for the life you have.

When you live from that place, "more" no longer tempts you. You know what matters. You know what enough feels like. And you finally have the strength to protect it.

Because sometimes the smartest thing you can do for your financial future is stop chasing what you already have.

TWENTY-THREE

Show Up More Financially

You have reached the end of this journey, but in truth, this is where it begins. Showing up financially is not about finishing a book or mastering a budget. It is about living differently. It is about stepping into each day with awareness, intention, and trust.

Money touches nearly everything in life, but it is never the whole story. It affects how you eat, where you live, what you stress over, and how you sleep. It can build peace or destroy it. It can strengthen relationships or strain them. It can free you or enslave you. The difference is not in how much you have. It is in how you show up.

Showing up financially means you stop drifting. You start paying attention. You know what comes in, what goes out, and why it matters. You take responsibility for your choices. You learn, you plan, you adjust, and you keep moving forward. It is not about perfection. It is about presence.

Most people live disconnected from their financial reality. They avoid it until it demands attention. They tell themselves it is too complicated, too stressful, or too late to fix. But avoidance is just delayed accountability. What you ignore today becomes the anxiety of tomorrow.

Showing up means facing the numbers, even when they make you uncomfortable. It means being honest about what is working and what is not. It means forgiving yourself for past mistakes and focusing on progress, not punishment. You are not your old decisions. You are who you choose to be now.

Every chapter of this book has been leading to that idea. Awareness. Automation. Stewardship. Generosity. Balance. Each one points to the same truth. Freedom does not happen by accident. It happens by design.

When you take ownership of your financial life, you take ownership of your future. You begin to see that money is not a separate category. It is part of your character. The way you handle it reveals how you handle everything else.

If you show up with discipline here, it will ripple into every area of your life. You will lead with more confidence at work. You will bring more peace into your home. You will experience less fear in moments of uncertainty. Because when you learn to manage something as emotional and practical as money, you strengthen the muscle of self-leadership.

Showing up financially is not about building wealth for its own sake. It is about creating stability that allows you to be present in the rest of your life. It gives you the space to think clearly, to give freely, and to live intentionally.

The goal is not to become obsessed with money. It is to build a healthy relationship with it. One rooted in clarity, peace, and purpose.

For some people, that will mean rebuilding from a difficult place. For others, it will mean refining what already works. Wherever you are, it begins with one simple decision: to be aware.

To stop letting money happen to you and start making money happen for you.

When you show up this way, you begin to notice something powerful. You start feeling lighter. The anxiety that used to follow you begins to fade. The chaos that used to surround your finances begins to calm. You start to experience order, not because everything is perfect, but because you are paying attention.

That attention creates peace.

You will not always get it right. You will overspend sometimes. You will make a bad investment, forget a payment, or wish you had done something differently. That is part of the process. What matters is that you stay engaged. You learn from it. You keep showing up.

Because that is what growth really is—returning to what matters, again and again.

As you move forward, remember what we have built together here. You learned that money is not just math. It is emotion, belief, and behavior. You learned that automation protects progress, that compounding rewards patience, and that freedom begins with clarity. You learned that wealth is bigger than numbers and that generosity is the proof of peace.

You also learned that more is not always better, that enough is sacred, and that systems create sustainability. You learned that stewardship outlasts success.

All of that wisdom only matters if you live it.

Showing up more financially does not mean you will never feel stress again. It means you will handle stress differently. You will face it with calm, not chaos. You will know that even when things get tight, you have structure, discipline, and faith to guide you. You will understand that your peace does not depend on your paycheck. It depends on your perspective.

Money will always come and go, but peace is something you can build. It is not fragile. It is earned through small, steady acts of responsibility. Through moments when you choose to pause instead of panic. Through quiet decisions that no one else sees.

Those moments are how you build legacy. They are how you become someone your family can depend on. Someone who leads with wisdom, not worry. Someone who leaves things better than they found them.

Because in the end, showing up financially is not just about you. It is about what your presence creates for others. Your calm becomes their confidence. Your structure becomes their safety. Your generosity becomes their hope.

That is the full circle of financial maturity. It starts with self-awareness and ends with service.

You do not need to have it all figured out to start. You only need to be willing. Every step you take toward clarity builds momentum. Every moment you choose intention over impulse builds peace. Every time you align your money with your values, you build freedom.

You are already capable of that kind of leadership. You do not need permission. You just need commitment.

So take a breath. Look at where you are. Then take the next right step.

Pay attention. Adjust when needed. Keep showing up.

Because this is how financial peace is built. Not in leaps, but in layers. Not in perfection, but in progress.

And when you keep showing up more financially, your life will begin to reflect what you have been working toward all along— freedom that feels peaceful, wealth that feels meaningful, and success that feels whole.

That is the life you have been building.

And it begins today.

www.ingramcontent.com/pod-product-compliance
Lightning Source LLC
Chambersburg PA
CBHW071222090426
42736CB00014B/2935